Hand Spinning
&
Natural Dyeing

By Claire Boley

HAND SPINNING & NATURAL DYEING

Published by The Good Life Press Ltd. 2011

ISBN 978 1 90487 1965

A catalogue record for this book is available from the British Library.

Published by
The Good Life Press Ltd.
The Old Pigsties
Clifton Fields
Lytham Road
Preston
PR4 oXG

www.goodlifepress.co.uk
www.homefarmer.co.uk

Cover design by Rachel Gledhill

Hand Spinning
&
Natural Dyeing

By Claire Boley

The Good Life Press LTD

CONTENTS

INTRODUCTION

ACKNOWLEDGMENTS

I wish to thank the British Wool Marketing Board for the details they have allowed me to use. Photographs were kindly supplied by Fiona Sloan of the Black Welsh Mountain Sheep Breeders, Louise Smith of the Jacob Sheep Society, Di Webb of the National Sheep Association (Dorset Horn), Sheila Leech of the Wensleydale Long Wool Breeders Association, Amanda Hannaford (www.mandacrafts.co.uk for the photos of the whorls), John Arborn, Arborn Textiles and Alison Hughes at the Somerset Rural Life Museum, Glastonbury, for allowing me to photograph her at work, and finally to The Good Life Press for having faith in me to write this book.

And last but by no means least my husband, Terry, for giving me space and supplying me with endless cups of tea. Thank you.

INTRODUCTION

As a young child I would sit spellbound watching my grandmother knitting for the family. As I was so fascinated she suggested she should teach me. Using commercial wool I knitted scarves for my teddy bears and dolls, and by the time I was 13 years old I was knitting jumpers for myself by following patterns.

Later, like millions of people in the 70s, I watched The Good Life series on the television and I will never forget Tom Good's pea green suit. Tom spun the yarn from the fleece from his own sheep. The green colour came from nettles that he brewed with Barbara's help. And so my eyes were opened to the world of natural dyeing and hand spinning.

Spinning is one of the most ancient of crafts and evokes early memories of fairy tales, magic, folklore and mystery. There are few things as satisfying as seeing a yarn that has been spun from a fleece, especially having produced it yourself, and I hope reading this encourages you to take up this ancient craft and to be as enthusiastic as I was when I spun my first yarn.

This book takes you through the complete process of spinning, explaining how to hand spin using your fingers, a drop spindle and a spinning wheel. It also guides you through spinning different types of yarns, from the basic to the elaborate, and how to dye your yarn, and here I share some of my recipes for producing the most wonderful colours, often using plants which grow in your own garden.

I have enjoyed many years of hand spinning and natural dyeing and have been privileged to be a full member of The Somerset Guild of Craftsmen, designing my own knitwear, holding workshops and solo exhibitions across the South West of England, and for this I am so grateful to the craft and what it has given to me. If this book encourages you to take up spinning and to experience anything like the immense pleasure it has brought me then I shall feel immensely proud, and happy that the craft's long history will continue into the 21st century.

So let's spin!

Claire Boley 2011

Note - Both metric and imperial measurements are mentioned throughout the book. One or the other should be used, but not both.

Chapter 1
SHEEP & FLEECE

Selecting A Fleece For Hand Spinning

Wool is the natural protection for sheep against the weather, allowing a normal body temperature to be maintained. The oil in the wool stops the wool getting water logged as the rain runs off the wool fibres. This also stops the wool from matting and is slightly oily to touch.

Under the surface of the sheep's skin there are pear shaped sacs known as follicles which grow the wool. The fibres are made up of a mass of soft elongated cells, and forcing these cells through the mouth of the follicles shapes them into round cells of wool fibre. The outside cells are flattened to form the scales of the fibre surface. The oil from the sebaceous gland lubricates the cells as they move along. As soon as the cells come into contact with the air they harden and form wool fibres. This is a continuous process for the sheep throughout its life. With the formation of new cells at the bottom of the follicles, the existing cells are pushed further out.

The domestic sheep is sheared each year, and for centuries the resultant fleece has been used by us for clothing. The wool provides warmth as air is trapped around the fibres and acts as an insulation. The wool also absorbs water vapour, which heats up and warms the trapped air around the fibres. As woollen fibres are wavy and not straight there are natural 'gaps' in between the fibres which trap even more air to add to the warmth and insulation of the natural woollen material.

The name given to groups of fibres growing in the same direction is a 'staple' or a 'lock'. These vary in length considerably from breed to breed. The amount of waviness, or crimp as it is referred to, also varies in the staple and the type of fleece.

The quality of the wool is governed by the amount of crimps in the staple, ie the more crimps per inch, the finer the wool. The diameter is measured in microns, a micron being one thousandth of a millimetre. The quality of the wool is known as the 'count'. This dates back over 200 years to the worsted industry in Bradford, and is called the 'Bradford count'. This states how many 560 yard long hanks can be spun from one pound of fleece, ie 560 yds is a 1 count, 1120 yds spun is a 2 count (560 x 2) and a pound of wool spun to 35,840 yards (560 x 64) is a 64 count. The higher the number of hanks spun, the finer the quality of the wool.

The details over the page have been provided by the British Wool Marketing Board (B.W.M.B.). Established in 1950 it is a farmer run organisation responsible for collecting, grading and auctioning wool. It keeps information on all types, qualities and characteristics of the entire fleece yield of the United Kingdom and Northern Ireland.

If you keep 4 or more sheep you have to register with the B.W.M.B. There are 53,000 registered sheep producers in the UK with over 60 breeds of sheep in the British Isles. This is more than in any other country in the world.

Different types of wool with different classifications.

British Wool Fleeces For Hand Spinners

The following range of fleeces have been specially selected by the British Wool Marketing Board to cover a wide range of hand spinning requirements.

TYPE NO. & DESCRIPTION	STAPLE LENGTH	MICRON COUNT	HANDLE	COLOUR	WEIGHT
Fine hog wool white	10-12cm	32.0	soft	White	2-3kgs
Fine wool white	7.5-10cm	33.7	soft	White	2-3kgs
Fine wool coloured	7.5-10cm	32.9	soft	Grey/Black	2-3kgs
Romney Kent	10-12.5cm	33.0	medium	White	3-4kgs
Leicester Cheviot cross hog	15-18cm	31.4	soft/medium	White	3-4kgs
Leicester Cheviot cross ewe & wether	12.5cm	34.5	soft/medium	White	3-4kgs
Jacob	7.5-10cm	32.8	soft	Piebald	2-3kgs
Masham	10-25cm	35.9	Medium/Harsh	White	2-3.5kgs

Fine cross hog (Blue faced Leicester cross)	15-23cm	29.0	soft	White	2.5-3.5kgs
Blue faced Leicester	12.5-15cm	26.1	soft	White	2-3kgs
Masham coloured	10-15cm	33.3	medium /harsh	Dark Grey	2.5-3.5kgs
Coloured Blue faced Leicester	12.5-15cm	26.1	soft	Black /Grey	2-3kgs
Wensleydale	20-28cm	33.6	smooth	white	3.5-4.5kgs
Cheviot	7.5-12.5cm	30.1	soft	White	2-3kgs
Shetland white	5-10cm	29.9	soft/silky	White	1-2kgs
Shetland moorit	5-10cm	29.9	soft/silky	Brown	1-2kgs
Welsh black	5-7.5cm	32.3	soft/ medium	Black	1-2kgs

The above information is supplied only as a guide, as each fleece is unique and may vary slightly.

11

LEFT Naturally coloured types: Jacob, Herdwick etc. with hundreds of cross breeds.

BELOW Shortwool and down type:
Dorset horn, Shetland

BELOW Mountain and hill type: Black Welsh mountain, Cheviot etc.

RIGHT Long wool and lustre type:
Wensleydale,
Blue faced
Leicester etc.

Staple/Lock Length

5cm – for the experienced hand spinner and suitable for woollen spinning.
7.5-10cm – recommended for beginners and suitable for woollen spinning.
12.5-18cm – for the experienced hand spinner and suitable for worsted spinning.
8cm+ – better suited for the experienced hand spinner.

Handle

Soft-medium – suitable for spinning apparel fabrics.
Medium -harsh – suitable for tweeds, coats & upholstery fabrics.
Harsh – suitable for upholstery & floor coverings.

It is possible for a wool spinner to buy a fleece direct from the B.W.M.B. for their own use. The board will help select the type of fleece that is required for a specific purpose. The address of the nearest office can be found in the yellow pages. When telephoning about buying a fleece, state the type required, approximate weight (as they differ considerably), staple length, and also let them know what you require the fleece for, ie felting, weaving, knitting etc. so that the board may be able to sort out a few for you to look at when you arrive. Ask if the fleece can be opened up so that its condition can be seen properly. Remember also to think colour. Different shades of brown, black, and grey are available in addition to cream, along with the Jacobs which have different shades of brown and cream in the one fleece.

If you are a beginner to hand spinning, buy a fleece with a staple length of 10-13cm (4-5 inches). This is the length from the root to the tip. A suitable fleece would be from a Cheviot sheep. Cheviots originally came from the Cheviot hills bordering England and Scotland. It has an average staple length of 10cm (4 inches), and a count of 48-50, with the wool varying from coarse to fine. Alternatively the Dorset horn, one of England's oldest breeds with an average staple length of 8-10cm (3-4 inches) with a count of 54-58, has one of the highest quality fleeces in the UK. It is very white, even before scouring, and is completely free of kemp (see page 15).

Sometimes you may be offered a fleece from a smallholder who keeps just a few sheep. If this does happen choose the fleece yourself, and if possible have a look at the fleece while it is still on the sheep. If you like it, get the owner to keep it for you.

Fleece is usually sheared during the months of May and June in the south of England and later in the north, ie July and early August.

If shearing is delayed a stressed sheep can lose its fleece by rubbing itself against posts, stone walls, or tree trunks. The fleece can weigh over 5kg depending on type, so it can feel very uncomfortable. The new wool will also start to grow, and when shearing does take place the shearer may be shearing away some of the next year's growth. To avoid this happening it is best to shear at the same time each year, especially if the fleece is to be used for hand spinning. Some farmers shear their sheep in the winter and after shearing these sheep are confined to the indoors. A freshly shorn sheep needs protection from the elements as it takes up to six weeks for a fleece to regrow sufficiently to provide effective insulation. A freshly shorn sheep requires more feed to maintain their normal body temperature, especially if shorn in the winter months.

It must be noted that if a 'winter fleece' is bought it will contain less lanolin, so both spinning and sorting will be more difficult as the fleece will not cling together.

Wool spun from a freshly sheared sheep, ie one shorn within the past week or so, is the easiest to spin, as the grease from the fleece has not had a chance to dry out and the staples are open. This makes the sliding and overlapping process in spinning with either a drop spindle or spinning wheel easier.

What To Avoid When Choosing A Fleece

Check the condition of the fleece before buying. If possible take a staple and hold it tightly with the tip between the first finger and thumb of one hand, and the root between the first finger and thumb of the other, and pull. If the staple breaks do not buy it as this may mean the sheep has been ill, has had malnutrition or a poor winter, thus weakening the fleece. This will also mean that the fleece may not stand up to combing or carding without the fibres breaking.

Although a farmer's individual dye marks usually wash out, the 'tupping' marks left behind by a ram are difficult to remove. I recommend that the fleece, or any parts of the fleece with these markings, are avoided.

Double cuts are tiny nips of wool which can be found on the underside of the fleece. They are the result of the shearer making a second pass over the fleece when shearing, or they could be next year's growth. In excess both can cause a problem when carding and spinning and should be removed when sorting the fleece if an even yarn is required.

Bright yellow stains caused by urine and infection will not wash out.

Over-dry and weathered tips are caused by the sun and sometimes harsh weather conditions. This affects the fleece, making the staples weak and causing them to break during preparation, ie when carding or combing.

Avoid fleeces which are matted, felted, or are very dry. These things make it very difficult to separate the fibres out before hand spinning.

Kemp is a thick, hairy, chalky coloured fibre in a cream fleece. It can be reddish in colour. It is usually found on sheep that are bred in the wet areas of the country, and in excess can be the result of poor breeding. Fleeces with kemp should be avoided if they are to be used for dyeing as the kemp will not take up the colour due to the medulla that is present.

Yolk comes from the sheep's glands and is situated on the wool fibres. It is a yellow mixture of grease and suint, and at certain times of the year it can become hard. With care it may wash out but the hard pieces should be avoided when spinning.

Mycotic dermatitis is a fungal skin disease which causes hard lumps and discolouration in the fleece.

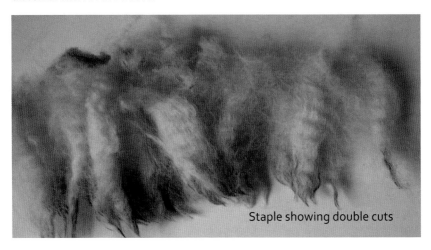

Staple showing double cuts

Fleece Sorting

Fleece sorting is the dividing up of the different parts of the fleece, and it is critical to get this right. If using just one fleece for a piece of work you need to make sure that there is a consistency in both colour and evenness. If different parts of the fleece are used it may spoil the appearance if different areas of a fleece differ considerably in texture. If using two fleeces for one project, make sure that they both have the same length staple and the wool comes from the same part of the fleece.

First release the neck band which is securing the fleece, unroll it to its full length, and open out each side. The fleece should have the tips of the wool locks facing upwards and the fibres that were closest to the sheep before

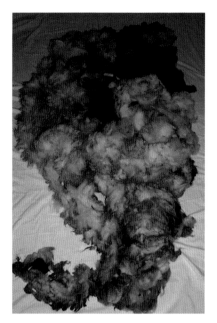

Jacob fleece.

shearing facing the floor. It should be quite easy to see which is the tail end of the fleece as the dirty, soiled area will be present around the tail together with the coloured tupping marks. The farmer's marks will also be on the back, usually at the tail end.

If the fleece has been stretched, shape it so it looks similar to the sorting diagram opposite.

1   **Extra diamond** feels finer, and is greasier to the touch.

2.   **Diamond** has a shorter staple and is lacking in natural oils so is quite dry, caused by bleaching by the ultra-violet rays of the sun and exposure to different weather conditions.

3.   **Prime** takes the worst of the weather and the fibre is often thinner and dryer. If this part is not too dirty it will be suitable as a coarse yarn or for mixing with either other fibres or different coloured fleeces.

4. ***Skirting*** is the short wool around the belly, the matted wool around the neck and the dirty and stained wool around the legs. All of this should be removed and discarded as it is usually too dirty and matted to use. At the same time remove the double cuts that can be seen on the under side of the fleece.

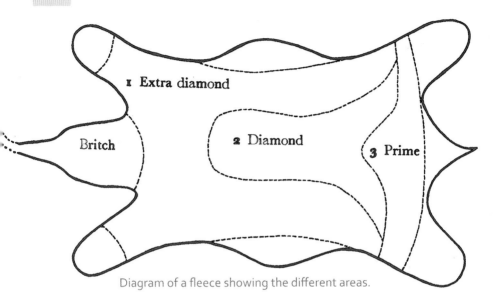

ı **Extra diamond**

Britch

2 **Diamond**

3 **Prime**

Diagram of a fleece showing the different areas.

Tip!

Never store fleeces in plastic bags as they will sweat and go mouldy.

Whether fleeces are scoured or left 'in the grease' (see page 19) when they are being stored, they still need to breath and should be put into hessian sacks or pillow cases. The fleece should be dried if it feels damp, and all of its skirting removed before going into storage. Label the storage bags, naming the type of sheep, date of shearing, and if it has been divided up, the names of the different qualities. The fleece should be stored in a cool area where the temperature does not fluctuate, so not the roof space in a house as it gets far too hot in the summer and the fleece will dry out and may felt. Make sure the fleece is checked occasionally when in storage for both dampness and moths. If the fleece is looked after correctly it can be kept and used at a later date, ie in a year's time.

Scouring

Scouring is the term for the removal of dirt, grease etc. from the fleece by thorough washing, leaving the fleece in a clean, grease free state ready for spinning or dyeing.

You will notice that when the fibre is in water it has a long range reversible elasticity. This means it is possible to stretch wool fibre one hundred per cent, ie 7cm (3 inch) fibre will stretch to 14cm (6 inches) in water. It will return to its orignal 7cm (3 inches) once it has dried. This can be repeated many times until the fibre becomes worn and then the length will be less than its original length.

The best way to approach scouring is the same way as washing woollens. Make sure that the fleece is not put into extreme temperatures of water and is not agitated as this will cause it to felt

After removing as much vegetation as possible from the fleece by hand and opening up the matted and weathered tips, put some warm water in a large bucket with soap suds that are suitable for wool, ie Lux or Dreft. Make sure that the suds have dissolved before adding the fleece to the water as the suds may cling to the fleece and remain after the fleece has dried, making it difficult to spin into a yarn.

Allow the fleece to soak for a while in the bucket to release the dirt. Drain the water from the fleece and prepare a second bucket, making sure the water is at the same temperature as the first. Leave the fleece to soak as before but for a longer period of time, ie half a day. Unless a third bath is required rinse the fleece in clear water - again at the same temperature. The fleece is now ready to dry naturally outdoors on either a net frame or in an onion bag so the air can circulate. It should always be remembered that the fibres can be damaged by extreme temperatures, so while the fleece is drying it needs to be put in the shade away from direct sun.

It is important to be as thorough at this stage as possible. If any grease is left in any of the scoured fibres that are to be used for dyeing, the finish will be uneven.

Preparing Scoured Wool For Hand Spinning

All of the natural oils will have been removed by scouring the fleece. It is sometimes beneficial to put the oil back into the wool for easier spinning, especially if you are a beginner or you find the fleece is extremely dry.

Add oil by using a house plant sprayer containing a mixture of an emulsion of 2 parts olive oil and 1 part water. Avoid using corn or vegetable oil as the fleece will become sticky, and these oils often stain the fibres and will not wash out. Lightly spray the scoured fleece with this emulsion just before you start spinning as an artificially oiled fleece will become rancid if left. Instead of using a sprayer some spinners put a small amount of olive oil on their finger tips just before spinning the scoured fleece. More experienced spinners do not find it necessary to replace the oil at all.

Occassionally it may be necessary to add an emulsion (1 part olive oil and 1 part water) to a fleece that has not been scoured due to the fibres being so dry - this should also be applied just before spinning is to commence.

Before spraying any fleece with the emulsion, think how much of the fleece you are going to spin at any one time. You do not want to discover the fibre has gone rancid before you get a chance to spin it.

After spinning the fleece into yarn, remove the emulsion by washing the yarn in warm, soapy water as soon as possible.

Spinning 'In The Grease'

I recommend if you are a beginner to hand spinning that you learn to spin 'in the grease'. By leaving the natural lanolin in the fleece it makes it much easier with the sliding and drafting of the fibres when using either a drop spindle or a spinning wheel especially if the sheep has been shorn in the last few weeks.

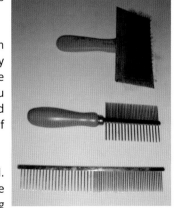

Once the fleece has been spun into a yarn it will be almost impossible to remove any debris that may still be present. Therefore before spinning a yarn 'in the grease' you should tease and open up the locks by hand or with a wool or dog comb to remove most of the vegetation and dirt.

Hold the lock by the root in the left hand. With tips away from the body, smooth out the fibres with the right hand fingers or by using the comb, then reverse the lock and repeat the process.

Different combs used for combing staples.

It is possible to spin a woollen yarn 'in the grease' by carding the fleece first (see Chapter 4) and also a worsted type yarn. (see Chapter 5).

When hand spinning straight from the fleece, the wooden parts of the wheel will get covered in grease from the spinner's fingers. The spun yarn going through the orifice and around the hooks on the 'U' shaped flyer will cause these parts also to get covered. The orifice will become blocked and will need cleaning out regularly, otherwise the diameter will get smaller and eventually only fine yarn will be able to pass through. When spinning the fibre may get caught up on the greasy hooks, causing the spun yarn to get trapped between the bobbin and the spindle. This can be alleviated by regular cleaning. I recommend using sugar soap to clean both the steel and the wooden parts of the wheel. It is a very good all round detergent and does not leave a smell like some other detergents.

If hand carders have been used with fleece 'in the grease' they will get extremely dirty and will be difficult to clean. The best way to clean hand carders is by using a dog comb to remove the waste fibre. Alternatively, hold the carders one in each hand, both in the same direction and with the wire hooks facing each other. Move one across the other to remove the waste. Do not wash the carders as they will be difficult to dry and may rust.

Using scoured wool with a wheel that has been used for spinning 'in the grease' will not help the clean yarn which may get covered in grease and could need washing again. Bearing all of this in mind it is a good idea, if possible, to have two spinning wheels and two pairs of hand carders.

1 spinning wheel for scoured fleece and commercial tops - clean spinning
1 spinning wheel for spinning direct from the fleece - dirty spinning
1 pair of hand carders for clean carding
1 pair of hand carders for dirty carding

Chapter 2

SPINNING WITH A DROP SPINDLE OR JUST YOUR FINGERS

Ceramic whorls by courtesy of Amanda Hannaford

Bronze whorls by courtesy of Amanda Hannaford

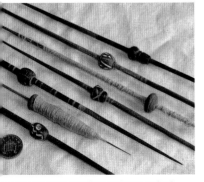

spindles by courtesy of Amanda Hannaford

The earliest form of spinning was finger spinning which was followed by the use of the spindle. Drop spindles have been around for centuries and have been found on archaeological sites dating back to 3000BC, when the shafts were made from wood or bone and the whorls from wood, ceramic or stone.

Spinning with a drop spindle is an ideal way of learning the basic principles of hand spinning. While using a spindle you can get used to the feel of the wool, learn how to judge the correct amount of twist, and improve your drafting technique before spending money on a spinning wheel. Some spinners only ever use a spindle and never move on to using a spinning wheel. It is a very convenient tool as you can walk around while using it. When the spindle is not in use it can still be carried around in a bag as it is very light and small.

Making A Drop Spindle

A very simple temporary drop spindle can be made from a 30cm (12inch) straight twig from a hedgerow. The whorl (the weight) can be made from a potato or an apple, with a hole put through the middle. The twig is used as the shaft. The end of this is put through the

Parts of a modern spindle.

Alison Hughes spinning with a temporary spindle.

hole in the whorl which is at the bottom end of the shaft.

There are 2 types of spindle readily available; a low whorl, known as a drop spindle, has the whorl at the bottom end of the shaft, making it heavy and too slow to spin a thin yarn. The other spindle has the whorl at the top end of the shaft. This rotates faster and is ideal for spinning fine yarns. It is important to have the right weight whorl and spindle for the yarn that is to be spun. A thick yarn is spun from a fleece with a long staple and will need a spindle with a heavy whorl. If you wish to spin a fine yarn, use a Shetland fleece with a lighter whorl.

These days both types of spindles can either be bought from specialist craft shops for a few pounds or can be made very easily from a narrow 1cm (¼ inch) piece of dowellling rod, (known as the shaft), 30cm (12 inches) long.

A hook is screwed into the bottom end of the shaft with a notch cut out 2.5cm (1 inch) from the top end of the shaft. The shaft is used as the bobbin for winding on the yarn once it has been spun.

At the bottom end of the shaft there should be a piece of round wood (the whorl) the size of a toy wheel 7.5cm (3 inches) across by 2cm (¾ inch) deep, with a hole in the middle that the shaft can go through. This is placed 2.5cm (1 inch) from the end and is used as a weight.

Spinning With A Low Whorl Spindle

* When using a spindle with a low whorl take a long piece of commercial yarn as the leader and tie this on the shaft just above the whorl. If the yarn should slip, secure it by taping it to the shaft. Hitch the leader yarn around the hook that is on the underside of the whorl, then take the leader up and over the whorl and loop it into the notch at the top of the shaft, allowing at least 30cm (12 inches) of leader yarn beyond this point for joining to the fibre. Take the lock of the fleece that is 'in the grease' and has been teased and separated by hand and overlap a few of the fibres from this lock on to the last 15cm (6 inches) of leader yarn. Hold the leader yarn with the lock over the back of the right hand and with the drop spindle hanging free, grasp the whorl with the left hand and twist it clockwise (a Z twist), immediately drawing down a few of the fibres onto the first few centimetres of the leader yarn. Twist the spindle again, making sure

that it is always spinning in a clockwise direction, and each time drawing out more fibres using the fingers and thumbs of both hands.Continue to do this, making a short length of spun yarn each time. When the spindle with the spun yarn reaches the floor, unhitch the yarn from the spindle and wind it onto the shaft just above the whorl.

Using the length of newly spun yarn from the shaft as the leader, rehitch it as before, leaving about 30cm (12 inches) of yarn at the top of the spindle so the spinning process can be repeated. When the shaft is full - this will be when it is difficult to maintain a spin - stop spinning. Remove the yarn by winding it into a ball.

Repeat this process once more from *
so there are 2 balls of single spun yarn ready to be plyed.

Spinning with a drop spindle.

Winding a single yarn onto a spindle.

Spinning With A Top Whorl Spindle

When spinning with a top whorl spindle, the whorl is positioned 2.5cm (1 inch) from the top of the shaft. This spindle can be made the same way as the low whorl, but the hook and whorl are positioned at the top end of the shaft. I have found that it is possible to use the same spindle, as discussed above, but by turning it up the other way.

When spinning a single yarn with a top whorl spindle, tie the leader yarn onto the shaft, under the whorl. Take this yarn up over the whorl, then pass it through the hook at the top. Join the leader to the fibre just as you did with the low whorl spindle, but instead of turning the whorl when beginning to make a yarn, turn the shaft instead, in a clockwise direction. Continue as it says for spinning with the low whorl spindle.

If there is insufficient twist the yarn will lack strength and may break.With too much twist too many fibres will be held together and the yarn may be too thick.

Plying A Yarn That Has Been Spun Using A Spindle

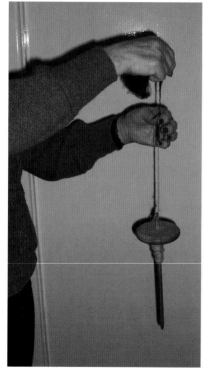

Spinning with a top whorl.

There are 2 ways to ply a yarn that has been spun in this way. It must be remembered that when plying any yarns they should be kept separate, either with your fingers or by threading the single yarns through a piece of wood with holes drilled through. This is so that the yarns do not get tangled and the tension is controlled.

24

Method One

* With the 2 balls of single yarn ready to ply, take the ends of both yarns in the right hand and put both balls of single yarn over the right shoulder into the shoe box which is placed on the floor behind the spinner. Holding the ends of the yarns in the right hand, tie them together on the shaft just above the whorl of the drop spindle. Take the 2 yarns, hitch them around the underside of the whorl and loop both yarns around the notch at the top of the shaft, just as you did for making the single yarn. Twist the drop spindle in an anti-clockwise direction (an S twist).

Plying using a shoe box.

Carefully allow the two separated yarns to feed and twist together as they come over the shoulder and through your fingers with equal tension. Stop when the spindle reaches the floor and wind the plyed yarn onto the shaft, just as you did with the single yarn. Repeat this until all of the plyed yarn is on the shaft. Remove the plyed yarn from the shaft by making it into a ball, ready to be made into a skein for scouring.

Method Two

Having filled two shafts on two drop spindles with single yarn, take an empty shoe box and make two holes in the lid, big enough for the shafts with the yarn to stand and fit in without moving.

Plying from the shafts of the spindles.

Put this box on the floor with the yarn and two shafts in position, with the whorls removed.

Take the two yarns and, with the empty spindle, repeat from method 1*.

Variations On Handling The Fibres When Spinning With A Spindle

ROLAGS

These are used to make a woollen yarn (see Chapter 4 'Carding'). Lay the rolag across the back of the left hand while holding onto the leader yarn, which is also being held in the left hand with the spindle hanging free. Take the tip of the rolag and overlap it by 5cm (2 inches) onto the leader yarn, before turning the spindle with the right hand in the clockwise direction, making a Z twist single yarn.

↑   Spindle spinning using a rolag.

↓   Using a lock.

COMBED LOCK

This can be spun into a semi-worsted yarn. First separate the fibres by combing the tips and the root of the lock with a dog comb. Take the combed locks and lay them across the palm of the left hand with the tips facing away from you, holding the roots in position with the thumb. With the leader yarn held in the right hand and the spindle hanging free, draft the fibres out from the right hand side with the right hand, and overlap them with the leader yarn by 7cm (3 inches) while turning the spindle in a clockwise direction.

STRAIGHT FROM THE FLEECE

These fibres may be of differing lengths. If an even yarn is required, separate out an area of the fleece with similar length locks before starting to spin.

Usually a textured yarn will be the result of spinning this way. Take a lock of the fleece, hold it by the root in the left hand, then tease and separate out the tips of the lock with the right hand so they do not cling together. Overlap the tip of the lock with the leader yarn by 7cm (3 inches), which is in the right hand with the spindle hanging free while turning the spindle in a clockwise direction. Spinning with a spindle this way is quicker and easier, especially if the sheep has just been shorn and a lot of lanolin is present in the fleece.

It is the choice of the spinner which hand is used for holding, twisting the spindle and drafting out the fibres, but whichever hand you decide to use, for each part of the process you should continue with the same hand for that particular yarn.

Problems When Using A Spindle

The yarn often breaks because there is not enough twist, or the scales on the wool will not catch together due to the fact that the fibres have not been teased out sufficiently before the spinning began, or the yarn that is being spun is far too fine.

The spindle starts to spin in the opposite direction because the spinner is concentrating on the drafting out of the fibres and has forgotten about the spindle which has simply stopped spinning one way and has automatically started to spin in the opposite direction, so the twist unwinds. With practice you will be able to keep an eye on both the drafting out and the direction of the spindle at the same time.

Finger Spinning

Finger spinning is the name given to twisting fleece into a yarn without using either a drop spindle or a spinning wheel but by a combination of twisting and drawing out of the fibres into a continuous line using only the fingers or the palms of the hands.

This is very time consuming and patience is paramount, but having said that, the only thing you need is a fleece which is in good condition with a lot of lanolin present. In the summer this should be easy to find if you live on a farm or smallholding and keep sheep, but if you don't you can always go to your local British Wool Marketing Board and buy one. The best type of fleece to use is one with a long staple not less than 8cm (3½ inches) in length. I would opt to use a fleece from either a Jacob or a Wensleydale sheep that had just been shorn.

Sometimes finger spinning is combined with hand knitting. A short length of twisted fibre can easily be turned into knitted stitches by twisting about 30cm (12 inches) of the fibre into yarn, then casting on a few stitches with a pair of knitting needles before twisting more fibre into yarn and making more stitches. It is possible to do finger spinning with either a rolag (see the Chapter 'Carding A Fleece') or a lock (another name for a staple). If a lock is to be used, the tips and roots need to be teased and separated out (see Spinning 'In The Grease').

Once the locks have been teased and separated, hold them in the left hand with the tips away from the body, ready to start twisting. The fibres are pulled out from the right hand side of the lock and twisted in a clockwise direction using the fingers of the right hand, or they can be rolled across the thigh with the palm of the right hand.

When using a rolag the fibres are drafted out from the tip just as they are when using a spinning wheel or spindle. Hold the rolag in the left hand and pull the fibres out with the right hand, twisting them in a clockwise direction to make a single yarn, the same as with the lock.

Once you have about 30cm (12 inches) of twisted yarn, wind it onto a piece of thin dowelling rod or make it into a ball. Continue to do this until you have enough single yarn for your requirements.

If the yarn is to be plyed, make 2 balls of singles, take the ends of the two balls and twist them carefully together in the opposite direction to the single yarn, thus making them into a single ball of plyed yarn.

After this fibre has been twisted into a yarn it should be scoured (see chapter 1

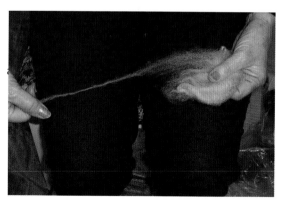

'Scouring') before being used for knitting or weaving. First it will need to be put into a skein as single or plyed yarn (see 'Making Skeins'). Make sure that the skeins are tied evenly and loosely in 3 places to stop the yarn from tangling while being scoured and dried.

Finger spinning with a lock.

After I have been finger

28

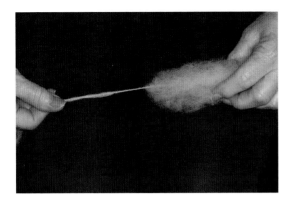

Finger spinning with a rolag.

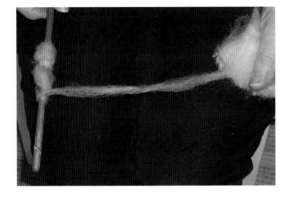

Winding yarn onto a piece of dowelling rod.

spinning or using a spindle, I have been known not to ply the yarn but to use it as a 'single', making it into a skein and scouring it. Once it has dried I have then wound the 'single' onto a commercial wool winder. The single yarn is then removed from the wool winder and used for knitting. I take the two ends of the yarn, one from the centre of the ball and one from the outside. These are both knitted together as if they had been plyed, making sure that the tension is the same for each yarn. I do not recommend using yarn this way for a large project as it may skew. Just use it for a sample, or to finish off a garment.

Making Skeins

If the yarn has been spun and plyed on a spinning wheel and needs to be made into a skein, the first thing to do is to slacken the drive band on a double band wheel, or the Scotch tension if using a single band wheel so there is minimum drag on the bobbin while it is still on the spindle of the 'U' shaped flyer. Remove the end of the yarn from the orifice so it is running free from the bobbin. Whichever type of wheel you are using, make sure that the length of yarn from the bobbin is held taut or it may twist back on itself. If the bobbin appears too loose, tighten the drive band or Scotch tension half a turn.

If the wool is not on the bobbin but in a ball, put the yarn into a bowl on the floor and continue to wind the wool into a skein as below. A skein can be made by using hands, forearm, the back of a dining room chair or a niddy noddy.

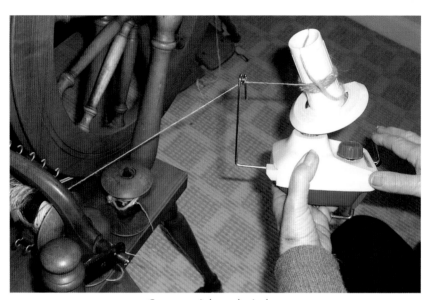

Commercial wool winder.

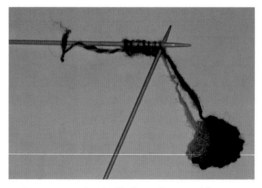

Knitting with a ball of wool wound from a commercial wool winder.

If your hands are to be used for making a skein, the first thing is to tie the end of the yarn around one of your thumbs, then holding your arms 60cm (24 inches) apart, start with help by winding the wool first around the hand that has the wool around the thumb, then take it across to the other hand/wrist and back again to the first hand. Continue to do this until all of the yarn has been used up. Before removing the skein from your wrists, tie the skein in 3 places so it does not tangle when washed.

Using the forearm, first bend your left arm. Wind the wool round the thumb of your left hand, and take the yarn up to the elbow and back down to the area between the thumb and forefinger. Continue to wind like this until all of the wool has been taken up into a skein. Tie it in 3 places, as before.

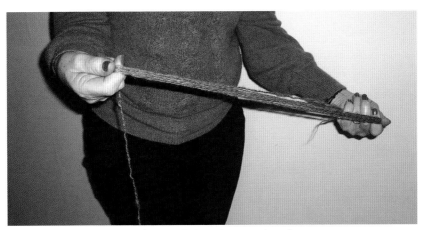

Making a skein using your hands.

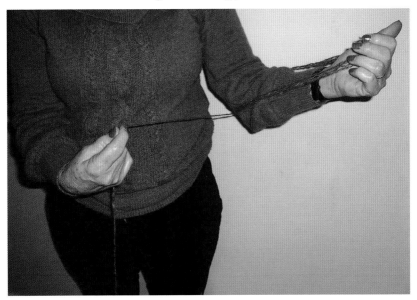

Making a skein using the forearm.

When using a dining room chair for this purpose, tape the end of the yarn to the side of the back of the chair securely, and wind the wool around the back of the chair until all of the wool has been made into a skein. Tie the yarn in 3 places, as before.

Using A Niddy Noddy

(see 'Making Or Buying A Niddy Noddy')

First attach the end of the yarn to one of the bottom arms of the niddy noddy. Holding the yarn in the right hand and the niddy noddy in the left hand, guide the yarn around the arms of the niddy noddy by taking the wool straight up to the top arm, turning the niddy noddy as you go, down to the bottom and up again, always remembering to turn the niddy noddy as you make the skein. Keep doing this until all of the wool has been used up. Before taking the yarn off the niddy noddy, tie the yarn in 3 places so it does not tangle when removed and scoured. If the yarn is to be dyed, after washing make sure the yarn is tied very loosely or the colour will be patchy due to the fact that the dye will not go under the ties.

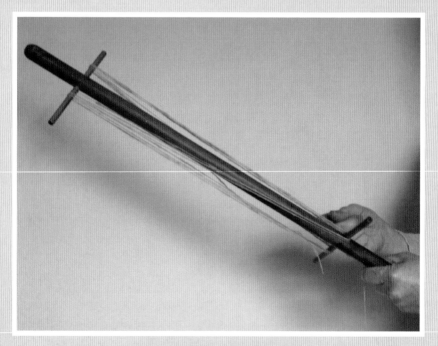

The yarn is now ready to be scoured and hung out to dry naturally in the garden.

Skeins That Have Been Spun From Unwashed Fleece

If the skeins of wool were spun from unwashed fleece they will need to be soaked before being scoured. The length of time needed for soaking the skeins depends on the dirt and grease present, and also the amount of twist in the yarn.

First fill a large bucket with enough warm water to cover the skeins. Do not agitate them and leave them to soak overnight. Remove them and hold them up to drain. Put them into more water of the same temperature and leave for a few more hours. Prepare the scouring bucket by filling it with warm water and adding soap suds. These should be dissolved before adding the skeins of wool. After leaving them for a few more hours in the scouring bucket, remove and drain them and rinse with care. Hang the skeins on a clothes line, preferably in the shade, straightening out each skein to remove any kinks. Some spinners put weights at the bottom of the skeins while drying the wool.

Making Or Buying A Niddy Noddy

A niddy noddy is for winding yarn into skeins. They can be bought from craft shops for just a few pounds or they can be made quite easily out of a length of broom handle and 2 small pieces of dowelling rod of different sizes. If one is bought from a craft shop it usually only comes in one size, but may come in different qualities of wood.

A normal length niddy noddy consists of a 66cm (26 inch) length of broom handle with two pieces of dowelling rod 15cm (6 inches) in length going through at right angles at each end of the broom handle. This makes the distance between the 2 cross bars 45cm (18 inches), making a 2 metre skein.

Small niddy noddys are quite handy if sample skeins of wool are needed. A good length is a 35cm (14 inch) length of broom handle with 2 pieces of dowelling rod measuring 10cm (4 inches) each. These also go at right angles at each end of the broom handle, making the distance 18cm (7 inches) between the 2 cross bars, so a 76cm (30 inch) skein can be made.

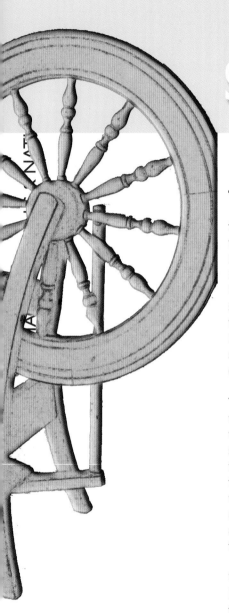

Chapter 3
SPINNING WHEELS

History Of The Spinning Wheel

The spinning wheel replaced the use of the drop spindle and one of the first was the great wheel, also known as the walking wheel or spindle wheel. This was first used in Europe in the 12th century and came over to England in the 14th century and was still in use in the 19th century when most families had 2 spinning wheels: a great wheel for spinning wool and a treadle wheel for spinning flax for linen. The reason for having the 2 wheels was so that the lanolin from the wool did not go onto the flax, making it difficult to spin.

The great wheel was operated by standing and walking backwards and forwards. The drive wheel was over 5 feet in height, with a very small spindle. The larger the drive wheel, the faster the spindle would turn, so the more twist the yarn would have per cm/inch. The spindle was mounted horizontally, with a cord going around once from the drive wheel to the whorl and tied, with another cord going around from the whorl to the spindle and tied.

When the great wheel was in use the fibre was held and drawn out by the left hand, while the drive wheel was being turned slowly in a clockwise direction using the right hand. Some spinners found it easier to use a stick for this process. At the same time the spinner would be walking backwards and away from the spindle head while drawing the fibre out. A leader yarn was still needed when using this type of wheel, and this was tied onto the far side of the empty spindle and spiralled up to the tip. The spinner then overlapped the fibre onto the leader yarn, as is the case with a modern treadle wheel, but by turning the drive wheel with the right hand and walking rather than sitting and treadling with the right foot.

The spun yarn was wound onto the spindle by first stopping the wheel, then turning the drive wheel backwards and unwinding some of the leader yarn that was already on the spindle. The drive wheel was turned clockwise again, winding the leader yarn followed by the newly spun yarn back onto the spindle, making a spiral. Once the winding on had finished, the end of the newly spun yarn needed to be positioned at the tip of the spindle so that the spinning could continue by using the spun yarn as the leader.

Alison Hughes spinning with the great wheel

The natural progression for spinning wool in the 16th century from the great wheel was the treadle/flyer wheel. As this wheel was a lot smaller it was easier to fit into the cottages, and the spinner could also sit down to operate it. They could treadle and rotate the drive wheel and spindle with one foot, thus having both hands free. This meant that the fibres could be drawn out with the left hand while being held in the right, or vice versa.

These spinning wheels are still popular today, either with a double drive band or a single drive band with a Scotch tension. It should be remembered that the main difference between the single and the double drive wheel is the method used for altering the tension and changing the bobbin. Before buying a spinning wheel for the first time it is advisable to ask as many experienced wool spinners as possible for advice and recommendations.

The Operation Of The Spinning Wheel

The operation of the spinning wheel begins by placing one foot over and in contact with the treadle. This is located under the table and is connected to two of the three spindle legs by means of the treadle bar. By moving your foot up and down in a continuous motion, it raises and lowers the foot-man via the treadle cord. On some models the foot-man and treadle cord are substituted by one stout cord. The top end of the foot-man is linked to the large drive wheel, via a crank on the drive wheel spindle. The spindle is supported by two uprights fixed to the table. It is the crank moving up and down and therefore turning the spindle which operates the main drive wheel. The up and down foot motion turns the main drive wheel, the drive band turns the whorl and therefore the flyer and the bobbin.

The outer rim of the main drive wheel is grooved and this carries a single or double drive band which drives the whorl (a small pulley) opposite the main drive wheel. The whorl is on the end of an assembly consisting of a flyer and bobbin. The bobbin is positioned within the arms of the 'U' shaped flyer. Guide hooks are screwed evenly along the 'U' shaped flyer arms, one row usually numbering six hooks on the top of an arm with the same number on the opposite arm, but on the underside. The whole assembly is mounted on a hollow spindle between two uprights called front and back maidens. These are fitted to a base called the 'mother of all'. This is adjustable using a wooden or steel screw, moving

the 'mother of all' either closer to or further away from the drive wheel. This adjustment alters the tension on the drive bands and therefore the rate at which the wool winds onto the bobbin: the tighter the drive band the faster the wool is drawn in.

Some spinning wheels have platforms on which the 'mother of all' is fitted, and also have a further arrangement on both main drive wheel uprights. This allows for a slight adjustment to the alignment of the drive band between the drive wheel and the whorl.

A length of commercial wool known as the leader is first threaded through the orifice (using a threading hook) of the assembly's spindle, coming out at the adjacent side hole known as the spindle eye between the flyer and the bobbin. This yarn is threaded along the flyer guide hooks and tied in position on the bobbin. After this the fibre that has been teased out by hand is taken up by the leader yarn and drawn through the orifice and spindle eye, and wound around the bobbin by continuous foot action on the treadle and the motion of the teased and twisted wool.

Things To Look Out For When Buying A Spinning Wheel

Expense is often an important factor when buying a wheel, but the most expensive is not always the best and may not be suitable for your needs. Avoid choosing a wheel because of the way it looks without actually understanding how it works First consider what type of yarn is going to be spun on a particular wheel: thick or thin or perhaps a little of each. Take a close look at the size of the orifice and the size of the hooks on the 'U' shaped flyer. The larger the hooks and orifice, the thicker the wool that can be spun.

The size of the drive wheel is important as spinning with a small drive wheel will require more treadling. It should be remembered that a wheel that has a ratio for spinning medium to bulky yarns may not spin fast enough to make a thin yarn.

Try to buy a wheel that has a 2 speed flyer/whorl as this enables the yarn to be spun at different speeds. Most wheels have upgrade kits with different flyer/whorl sizes, so if you buy a medium speed wheel and later decide that you want to spin thinner yarns, it should be possible to buy and replace the current flyer with a higher speed version and the appropriate bobbins and whorls. Jumbo flyers with jumbo bobbins are also available to spin bulky yarns.

Make sure you can understand the instructions if buying a new wheel, as most wheels come in kit form and will need to be put together. Included with the instructions should be the ratios of the wheel. If it is second hand, make sure there are instructions with the wheel, and if not, ask the seller for help, explaining that you are new to the craft. I recommend that you take a friend who is a spinner with you, especially if buying a second hand wheel, as you are not likely to know whether the wheel is correctly balanced or treadles smoothly, or if any of the parts are missing and how much they will cost to replace.

There are several types of spinning wheels on the market today. One of the most popular for beginners is the Ashford traditional which is saxony style. It comes with a double drive band or with a single band with a Scotch tension. Some Ashford wheels come with both and can be changed over from one to the other quite easily. The castle style is also popular, especially with spinners who wish to transport their wheel, the most popular being the Ashford traveller. This

Double band spinning wheel (Sleeping Beauty) showing parts

1. Double drive band

2. Drive wheel

3. Tension adjustment screw

4. Bobbin rack

5. Foot-man

6. Treadle

7. Saddle

8. Orifice and spindle eye

9. 'U' shaped flyer with bobbin in situ

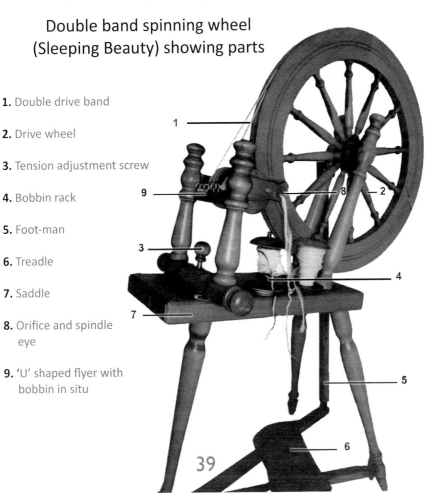

39

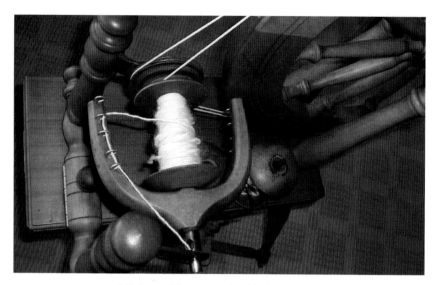

'U' shaped flyer on a double band wheel

style comes with both a double band and a single band with a Scotch tension. Some also have a double treadle operable with either both feet or just one foot.

The Flyer Ratio

Before buying, it is important to understand the drive wheel to flyer ratio, as this determines the speed of the wheel and how many twists per cm/inch go into the yarn.

Tie a piece of yarn onto the flyer and another onto the drive wheel and position the foot-man at the highest position on the drive wheel. With the drive band going around and across onto one of the whorls, turn the drive wheel very slowly by hand just one revolution, at the same time counting how many times the flyer turns during that single revolution. Then divide the circumference of the flyer/whorl into the circumference of the drive wheel.

The higher the ratio i.e about 20-1 has more twist, so a finer yarn can be spun. A wheel with low ratios, ie 4-1, will spin bulky yarns with less twist. If it is 10-1 it will mean that there will be 10 twists to 1 inch of yarn spun, to one turn of the drive wheel. If you hold the yarn back before it is allowed to go through the orifice to 2 turns of the drive wheel it will mean, with this particular wheel, that it will be a ratio of 20-1. If you allow 2 inches of yarn to go through the orifice to one turn of the drive wheel there will be 5 twists per cm/inch.

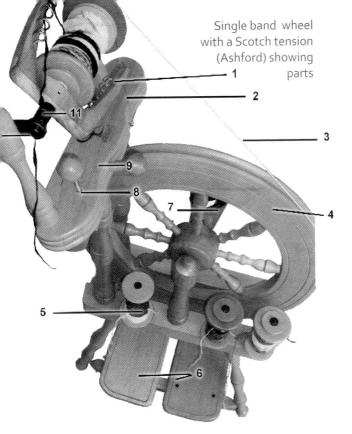

Single band wheel
with a Scotch tension
(Ashford) showing
parts

1. 'U' shaped flyer

2. Scotch tension
   - nylon thread

3. Single drive band

4. Drive wheel

5. Bobbin rack

6. Double treadle

7. Foot-man

8. Mother of all with
   tension adjust-
   ment for the drive
   wheel

9. Tension adjust-
   ment for scotch
   tension posi-
   tioned on the
   side of the
   mother of all

10. Orifice and
    spindle eye

Ashford traveller/castle wheel

A Double Band Spinning Wheel

This type of treadle/flyer wheel has a double drive band, which is a piece of string that is crossed over once, but runs twice around the drive wheel and spindle unit. The ends of the drive band are joined together by either sewing or by tying the string into a reef knot. The drive belt tension adjustment should be at the minimum setting when joining the ends of the band together. If it is not, the tension adjustment will not be available when the drive band stretches. Control and adjustment is possible by turning the tension adjustment screw. This moves the drive belt up and down, thus altering the tension and changing the speed at which the yarn winds onto the bobbin when spinning. It must be remembered that a tight drive band will draw the yarn in rapidly, so the yarn will have a low degree of twist. A slack drive band will draw the yarn in slowly and create a high degree of twist. Accurate adjustment is extremely important.

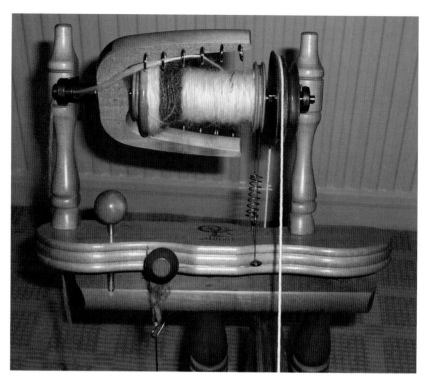

A secondary tension adjustment can be found on this wheel, and by transferring the drive band onto the smaller diameter spindle whorl, the yarn spun will be thinner and have more twist per cm/inch, and will accumulate rapidly onto the bobbin. When using a double band wheel it will be noticed that the wheel and the bobbin spin faster than the 'U' shape flyer.

Single Drive Band Spinning Wheel With A Scotch Tension

The Most popular wheel of this kind is the Ashford traditional or the Ashford traveller/castle wheel. The drive band for this wheel runs only once   around the drive wheel and spindle unit, but is tied in the same way as the double band wheel,

Top: 'U' shaped flyer with a Scotch tension. Bottom: Ashford traditional spinning wheel with a lazy kate.

either by sewing the ends together or by tying the string into a reef knot.

The Scotch tension has a wooden peg which is screwed into the side of the 'mother of all' with a nylon thread attached to it. The thread goes along and through the hook on the side of the 'mother of all', and the thread then goes up and over the bobbin rim to the small spring to which the nylon thread is tied. The spring is then attached to the hook positioned on the top of the mother of all.

Foot-man

The Scotch tension drives the bobbin. This tension is adjusted by turning the small wooden peg. The single drive band from the wheel drives the spindle and the 'U' shaped flyer by altering the drive belt tension adjustment. When spinning with this type of wheel it will be noticed that the bobbin is almost stationary and the yarn is laid onto the bobbin by the rotation of the 'U' shaped flyer. The 'U' shaped flyers on both spinning wheels have hooks on one side of each arm, enabling the spinner to distribute the yarn evenly onto the bobbin by moving the yarn along the hooks by hand. The size of the orifice and the closeness of the hooks gives an indication of the type of yarn the wheel can spin: a large orifice and wide spaced hooks will accept thick, bulky yarn, as well as a fine yarn.

The traditional Ashford from New Zealand with a lazy kate has been on the market since the 1940s and has been sold all over the world, mainly in kit form.

Threading A Double Drive Band Or A Single Drive Band Spinning Wheel With A Scotch Tension

First put the empty bobbin in position on the spindle. Take a long piece of commercial wool about 60cm (24 inches) in length as the leader yarn and tie the end securely onto the empty bobbin - if the yarn should slip, tape it onto the bobbin. Take the other end of the leader yarn by hand and put it around the first hook of the 'U' shaped flyer and run it along the bottom of all the

Fibres being taken up by the leader yarn

hooks until it reaches the spindle eye and orifice. Take the threading hook and insert it through the orifice into the spindle eye and out the other side. Pull the threading hook towards you with the yarn in situ, and back through the spindle eye and the orifice. You are now ready to start spinning.

Learning To Treadle

If you are a complete novice, practice treadling without any yarn. First put the foot-man in the 2 o'clock position as this helps to stop the drive wheel from turning anti-clockwise when you want it to turn clockwise, or vice versa. With the right foot on the treadle, and the right hand turning the drive wheel in the clockwise direction, you should now be treadling. Do this until you feel confident and are managing to get the spinning wheel to turn consistently in the same direction, ie clockwise. Once you have mastered this, take hold of the leader yarn that has been pulled through the spindle eye and orifice, and practice treadling while holding onto the leader yarn, but allowing this yarn to be taken up by the bobbin.

Getting Leader Yarn To Take Up The Fibre

This takes a lot of practice, as the hands and feet need to work together with the drive wheel, which should be turning in a clockwise direction at the same time, to make a Z single yarn First take a lock of the fleece and tease out the root and tips of the fibres using your fingers. Put these to one side (see Chapter

44

1 'Spinning In The Grease'). Next pull the leader yarn through the spindle eye and orifice as shown - threading a wheel - making sure that there is enough yarn available to use as the leader after it has come out of the spindle eye and orifice. I recommend a 30cm (12 inch) length..

Before setting the wheel in motion, allow a small amount of the tips of the teased fibres to overlap the side of the leader yarn by 7cm (3 inches). With the foot-man in the 2 o'clock position and the leader yarn held in the left hand, with the roots of the teased fibres held between the thumb and the first finger of the right hand, put your right foot on the treadle and start to rotate the drive wheel in a clockwise direction, using the right hand but still holding onto the fibres - you should now be treadling, and the teased fibres should be taken up by the leader and going through the orifice and spindle eye onto the bobbin. As these fibres are used up, more teased fibres will be needed to overlap onto the spun yarn, which is now being used as the leader.

If you are finding it difficult to co-ordinate your hands with your foot/feet, ask a spinning friend to help out. Perhaps he/she could do the treadling and you concentrate on joining the fibres to the leader yarn

Difficulties When Spinning On A Wheel

Difficulty in drafting	In the first instance it may be found that it is difficult to draft on correctly and also not quickly enough. Do not grip the rolag or lock too tightly, and do not hold the yarn back before it goes into the orifice as it will over twist. After succeeding to spin a continuous yarn, the quality will, with practice, start to improve.
Tying the leader yarn	When using a fresh bobbin, the leader yarn should be either tied securely onto the bobbin or taped in position - this will stop it from slipping.
If the wool disappears through the orifice onto the bobbin	Find the end by remembering which hook the yarn was last put around, and rub your fingers along that area of the bobbin as the drive wheel is turned slowly by hand.
Drive belt slipping	Adjust the tension using the tension adjustment screw. If this does not help, the belt may need replacing.

Over twisting	If the wheel has a double drive band and the yarn is over twisting (spiralling), or not winding on fast enough, tighten the tension adjustment half a turn, or tighten the Scotch tension half a turn, if you are using a single drive band wheel
Not enough twist	If the yarn is drawing in too quickly and there is not enough twist, slacken the tension adjustment half a turn on the double drive band wheel, or slacken the Scotch tension half a turn on the single band wheel.
The wheel becomes very stiff	If the wheel becomes very stiff when spinning and treadling is difficult, the drive band may be out of alignment with the flyer whorl. Check the maidens, making sure that they are parallel, and adjust them if necessary, or it could be that the 'mother of all' needs to be re-aligned.
Wheel turning the wrong way	When the wheel keeps turning in the opposite direction, it sometimes helps if the foot-man is put in the 2 o'clock position before starting to treadle. Altering the position of the foot that is being used for treadling also helps, but usually it is more practice with the treadling that is required.
Difficulty when joining the leader yarn to the fibre	This usually means that the fibre needs to be teased out more before joining it to the leader yarn.
The yarn isn't winding onto the bobbin	This could be because the leader is not threaded up correctly, or the yarn is too thick to go through the orifice and spindle eye. The yarn may be caught around one of the hooks, or it could have gone down between the bobbin and the 'U' shaped flyer onto the spindle, due to the fact that the wheel has turned the wrong way. The tension adjustment screw may need tightening if you are using a double band wheel. On a single band wheel it may be both the tension adjustment screw and the Scotch tension that need altering.

The fibre keeps falling apart

It could mean that there is not enough twist in the yarn. The spinner needs to treadle faster, and at the same time the yarn needs to be held back to get an extra amount of twist before letting it go through the orifice and spindle eye onto the bobbin.

Tension adjustment

When spinning on the wheel and the bobbin fills up, the tension needs to be altered. When using an empty bobbin the new yarn only goes a short distance around the bobbin 8cm (2½ inches) as it fills up you will find the yarn will be travelling further. If you spin the yarn at the same speed throughout without taking into account the distance the yarn has to travel as the bobbin fills, you will notice that the yarn has a high degree of twist at the start of the spinning but has less twist as the bobbin fills up. To keep the twist constant adjust the tension on the wheel.

The yarn keeps breaking and has too much twist

This means that the spinner is holding the yarn back for too long a time, and is also treadling too quickly before letting the yarn go through the orifice and spindle eye onto the bobbin. It can be corrected by treadling slower, and drafting in quicker.

The yarn is being pulled through too quickly

This means that the tension is too tight and needs to be loosened.

To avoid losing the spun yarn on the bobbin

When spinning has finished, wind a few inches around the front maiden. This will also prevent the yarn from untwisting. When the spinning is resumed, put a little more twist onto the end of the spun yarn (now the leader yarn), by treadling before joining the leader to the fibre.

Why is the wheel moving away while I am spinning?

Most probably the chair is too low and when treadling your foot is pushing the wheel away, or your foot is in the wrong position on the treadle.

Maintenance

A spinning wheel is a working tool and if it is treated well it will last for many years. Some new spinning wheels are bought stained with either polyurethane varnish or wood stain, while other wheels are bought without any stain and need linseed oil applied to preserve the raw wood and also to give the wheel a natural look.

Most wheels are bought in kit form, making it easier to stain before being put together.

When the fleece is being spun 'in the grease' on the wheel, clean the wood after every use with a little methylated spirit, then re-oil it if the wheel was originally stained with linseed oil. If it has had polyurethane varnish or wood stain applied, leave it alone after cleaning with the spirit.

All the moving parts should be oiled using a good sewing machine oil most days, especially if the wheel is being used regularly. If the wheel is not being used regularly, oil it before using it.

Inspect the drive band cord as it may stretch after one week of regular use. Undo the knot and tighten it up, or replace it if it appears worn through age. If you are using a single band wheel with a Scotch tension, check the nylon thread as well, and if worn, replace it with some fishing line, ie 40lb breaking strain. If the spring needs replacing an elastic band can be used.

Spinning wheels should be kept away from heated radiators and direct sunshine, as both may cause the wheel to warp, and the drive band cord may also become stretched.

A Chair For Hand Spinning

It is the spinner's own choice as to which type of chair is used, however, as you may be sitting at the wheel for several hours at a time, make sure that it is comfortable and suits your needs. I use a dining room chair with a high back, with a distance of 46cm (18 inches) from the floor to the seat, this gives a good working height in relation to the spinning wheel. On the seat I place a wedge shaped foam cushion as this positions me at a slightly forward angle, making it easy to treadle. If you sit too low, the pushing down action when treadling will cause the wheel to move forward.

Chapter 4
CARDING & COMBING FLEECE

Diagram of teasel comb.

Combing locks with a dog comb.

Before hand carders were invented, teasels (*Dipsacus fullonum*) were used for both carding and combing out the fibres. Teasels are plants that grow either in the hedgerow or can be cultivated in the garden by buying seeds from garden centres. They grow to a height of 4-6 feet, with prickly heads which in mid to late summer are a pinkish purple colour, or some times white. They dry to a shade of brown.

Once the teasels had dried they were put on a wooden frame, four teasel heads at the top with the stems coming down between six more heads and stems. All the teasels were fixed between two pieces of wood which held all ten stems in place, with a wooden handle coming down the centre of the frame.

Hand carding is essential for the production of a woollen yarn. Today it is prepared by first teasing the fibres out by hand, or by combing them out with a dog comb, then making them into a rolag by using hand carders. A woollen yarn is warmer than a worsted type yarn due to air being trapped between

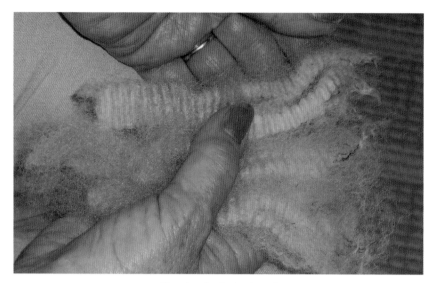

Teasing locks by hand.

the fibres while carding. It will be noticed that the carded fibres go round and around when spun from a rolag, instead of in a parallel line as they do when spun into a worsted type yarn from a combed lock or roving.

The fleece used for making rolags should have a staple length of less than 10cm (4 inches), as a longer staple will override the depth of the hand carder and a ridge will form, so when spinning takes place one side of the rolag may have a ridge going along the inside, making it difficult to spin.

A fleece with a staple length that is longer than 10cm (4inches) should be teased and combed out and used for spinning a worsted type yarn (see Chapter 5 'Spinning Techniques').

Combing Locks

Before carding can take place, the locks need to be teased out by hand, and this teasing out process is dependent on the condition of the fleece. If it is soft, open, and clean, only a little teasing will be required, but if the fleece has a lot of vegetation present it will need to be teased and combed out using a dog comb as the fibres will be clinging together in the affected areas (see Chapter 1 'Spinning In The Grease'). Remove any double cuts that may be present; these can be put aside to use with fancy yarns, or they can be disposed of. If there is a lot of vegetation and foreign matter present and it is difficult to remove, avoid this part of the fleece as it will only cause a lot of problems, one being that it will still be in the yarn after it has been scoured, so when it comes to using the yarn for a special project it will still be noticed.

The teased locks should be put into a basket in a loose mass to await carding. Do not press them down.

Hand carder on left thigh.

There are two types of hand carders: curved and flat. The preferred type is the spinner's own choice. By using the flat carders, more of the wire hooks can work against the opposing carder at any moment than with the curved type. The curved carders are better for the rolling action that is required for making the rolag after the carding has finished, but these cost a few pounds more.

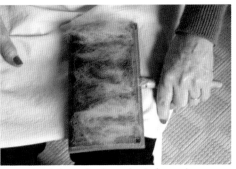

Applying a lock to the left carder.

Each carder consists of a piece of wood 20 x 10cm (8 x 4 inches) with a wooden handle. On the underside of the wood there is a piece of canvas with wire hooks attached. The wooden handle is on the back of the carder and is securely fixed to the main part to give adequate strength when carding the fibres.

Drawing right carder over the left carder.

After buying the hand carders it is advisable to apply linseed oil to the wood as this stops the grease from the fleece becoming absorbed into the wood, and it is also necessary to take the carders and label them both permanently left or right, as they will wear unevenly.

Transfering the fibre from the left carder to the right.

Method 1 Making a rolag.

Method 2 Making a rolag with fingers.

Before hand carding takes place, the spinner needs to decide whether the fleece is to be scoured before or after carding If it is scoured before it may be very dry and will need a little oil/water put back into the fibres by spraying before spinning. The advantage of scouring the fleece before is that most of the vegetation and foreign matter will have disappeared, so making carding cleaner (see Chapter1 'Sheep And Fleece - Scouring Fleece').

Hand Carding

Prior to any carding, put on an apron which will cover you down to the knees. This is simply to avoid your clothes getting covered in grease and vegetation.

✶   Put the left hand carder across the left thigh, holding the handle with the palm of the left hand with the wires facing upwards.

✶   With the right hand apply the teased locks firmly and evenly across the left carder, tips first, and draw them against the direction of the wire hooks, making sure that they do not go beyond the back of the hooks. If you wish you can put different coloured teased locks at even intervals on the carder instead of just a one coloured (ie cream) fleece.

✳ Take the right hand carder in your right hand with the wire hooks facing down. Draw this carder across the fibres which are on the left hand carder (this should still be in position on the left thigh and must not be held in the air) by lightly stroking the surface of the fibres. Repeat this action a few times until most of the fibres have been transfered to the right carder (making sure that the wires from each carder do not touch each other: if it seems like hard work the carders are not being used lightly enough, or there may be too much fleece on the left hand carder)

✳ The next stage is to transfer the remaining fibres from the left hand carder onto the right. Do not change the position of the hands on the carders, but turn the right hand carder over so the wire hooks are uppermost. With the bottom edge of the left hand carder (wire hooks facing down) over the bottom edge of the right carder, and with pressure, transfer the remaining fibres from the left carder to the right carder. When doing this it is necessary to keep the carders at a 60 degree angle as the fibre ends may get caught up and double back, causing a ridge of double fibres along the edge of the carder which will impair the rolag.

✳ Repeat this process, but from the right to left carder.

✳ The fibres are now ready to be removed and made into a rolag. To do this transfer the fibres from the left to right carder as before, but with less pressure. Continue to do this until the fibres appear light and airy and are lying free on the right hand carder.

Making A Rolag Method #1

✳ Place the left carder with the wire hooks downwards across both thighs and with the handle facing to the left. Put the fibre that has been carded onto the wooden back of this carder, and pat the fibre with the wooden side of the right hand carder. With the edge of the right hand carder, lift up the edge of the fibre - about 2.5cm (1 inch) - and press it down so it folds onto itself, then with the wooden side of the carder, lift the folded edge up and roll it across the remaining fibre from the right side to the left. This should result in a cylindrical roll known as a rolag. If you find this difficult, roll the fibre between the palms of your hands, but not pressing too hard on to the fibres.

Making A Rolag Method #2

✳ Place the right hand carder, wire hooks uppermost, with the fibres in position on the carder and the handle towards your body. The fibres are now ready to be rolled. Curl the fibres on the far side of the carder towards you using the thumbs and fingers of both hands, and continue to roll the fibres across the carder towards you, making them into a rolag as the fibres are rolled.

★   Once the rolags have been made they should be kept in a basket undisturbed, with the fibres full of air, and not squashed down. Refrain from pulling them out of shape. Try to make sure that the rolags are used within a day or so of being made. as the spinning will be easier and the fibre will slide more freely. Constant switching from carding to spinning causes lack of rhythm, and a less satisfying result. It takes a lot of time and practise to be able to make a good rolag. It should be done thoroughly, so all the fibres are intermingled, fluffy and full of air, otherwise you may as well tease the wool and forget the carding as poor spinning may be the result.

Faults When Hand Carding

It is important to make enough rolags to keep you spinning without having to switch from spinning to carding and back, as constant switching causes a lack of rhythm in the spinning, and you will get a less satisfying result.

Imperfectly rolled rolags cause problems when spinning a woollen yarn. Do not over card as this damages and breaks the fibres. Card lightly and transfer firmly.

Make sure all the locks are the same length and they are all facing in the same direction, with the tips facing the handle edge. Do not allow the fibre ends to project beyond the handle edge of the carder as a ridge may form due to the doubling over of the fibres when transferring from one carder to the other. When making a rolag, roll the carded wool evenly but firmly. If rolled too loosely, control when spinning will deteriorate.

Drum Carding

A drum carder is an easy machine to operate and is kinder to the hands than hand carders, especially if you have any kind of arthritis. Some are powered by an electric motor while others are operated manually by rotating a handle fitted to the spindle on the operating side of the large main drum which collects the carded fibre. Attached to the rear end of the spindle is a pulley, belt driving a second pulley which is fitted to a smaller diameter drum. The difference in

Rolag made from a batt.

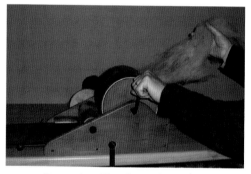

Removing fibre from the drum.

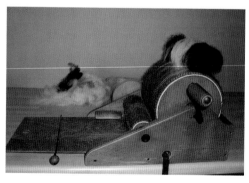

Coloured rolag from a batt.

pulley diameter will give a steady feed, so, as the handle on the large drum is rotated clockwise, fibre that has been laid on the pick-up shelf is automatically taken up by the in-feed smaller drum and transferred onto the main large storage drum. This is achieved by means of both drums being covered with carding cloth, which has wire hooks attached.

Before using the drum carder the fibres need to be teased out by hand, or with a comb. (see 'Combing Locks). It does not matter which end of the lock is picked up by the in-feed drum first, but it should be remembered to make sure that all of the locks are fed in the same way, either tip first or root first, and not a mixture. The pulling between the two drums straightens the fibres out and lays them on the wire teeth of the carding material on the large drum. When the large drum is completely full, remove the fibres by first running the metal wool removing pin along the seam of the carding cloth, and turning the handle in an anticlockwise direction with the left hand. Gently pull the fibres away from the wire teeth using the right hand, thus removing all of the fibres from the main drum.

The fibre will come away from the drum in a long strip which is called a batt. This can either be spun worsted style as a roving if the lock length is long enough, or if the lock length is less than 10cm (4 inches), the fibre can be made into a rolag and spun into a woollen yarn (see Chapter 5). The rolag can be made by breaking the batt crossways at 15cm (6 inches), then rolling the 15cm length by hand into a rolag.

A roving is made by pulling the batt apart lengthwise. Each batt should be around 61cm (24 inches) in length, so when it has been divided up into a roving it should be 243cm (96 inches) in length, and 5cm (2 inches) wide (see Chapter 5 'Spinning Techniques - Making A Roving').

Commercial Carding

These days you can send a fleece away to a mill to be carded commercially, but before doing this the fleece needs to be skirted and scoured. Some mills may scour the fleece too at an extra cost.

When carding the fleece by machine, the operator will put the clean wool fibres in to a scribbler which has coarse iron teeth. The fleece is brushed out and the fibres straightened, then transferred over to a series of rolling drums, each with finer teeth than the one before. When the fibre arrives at the last drum it will automatically be in a continuous sliver or a batt, ready to be either hand or

Commercial Carding

Empty scribbler at Cold Harbour Mill, Uffculme, Nr. Cullompton, Devon

Fleece that has been made into a sliver commercially and automatically being put into the bins at Cold Harbour Mill, Uffculme, Nr. Cullompton, Devon

Commercial Carding

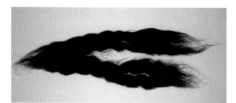

Sliver parted down the middle before being hand spun.

Rolags made from a commercial sliver.

Commercial batt from a british milking sheep

commercially spun into a yarn.

The hand spinner can either break off a 15cm (6 inch) length of the sliver which is 13cm (5 inches) wide, and roll it into a rolag and spin it semi-woollen, or it can be broken across at 61cm (24 inches) and made into a top by parting the sliver down the middle, and hand spinning it into a worsted type yarn

If the fibre comes out of the machine as a batt, it can be divided up and made into a roving and spun into a worsted type yarn (see Chapter 5 'Spinning Techniques - How To Make A Roving').

Different length locks.

Leader yarn tied onto the empty bobbin (birds eye view).

A Woollen Yarn

A woollen yarn is spun from a rolag using the long draw technique from a short stapled fleece. This should be less than 10cm (4 inches) in length. It can be spun into any thickness of yarn from fine to very thick by the spinner adjusting their own technique as well as adjusting the tension adjustment screw (see Chapter 3 'Spinning Wheels - Things To Look Out For When Buying A Wheel' and 'Drive Band And Flyer Ratio'). Air is trapped between these fibres when carding, making the spun yarn soft, very elastic and warmer than either a worsted or semi-worsted yarn (see Chapter 4 'How To Make A Rolag').

To spin a woollen yarn first tie the leader yarn on to the empty bobbin that is on the 'U' shaped flyer, and put the end of the leader yarn around the first hook on the flyer. Using the threading hook, pull the yarn through the orifice and spindle eye ready to join to the rolag.

Hold the leader tightly in the left hand, and using the right hand rotate the drive wheel clockwise one turn so more twist goes into the leader, before joining it to the rolag and treadling. Stop the wheel from turning, but still holding onto the end of the leader in the left hand and making sure that the extra twist is still in the leader. With the rolag in the right hand lay a few of the fibres from the tip of the rolag 6cm (2 inches) along the side of the leader, so the leader

59

Spinning a woollen yarn.

can take up the fibres from the rolag (see Chapter 3 'Joining A Leader'). With the leader and the spun yarn held between the thumb and first finger of your left hand and the rolag being held lightly between the thumb and first finger of your right hand, start treadling and drawing out the fibres to the right hand side with your right hand to a working length, ie 50cm (19 inches). While this is happening the left hand is holding the yarn tightly so it accumulates more twist, before allowing this twist to run up the drafted fibres to make a completed yarn. Release the tension of the right hand and let the yarn wind onto the bobbin. Both hands should now be near the orifice.

Hold the yarn tightly with the thumb and first finger of your left hand and let the twist from the wheel accumulate again, repeating the drawing out and twisting process as before.

When one rolag has been used up, another rolag should be joined to the newly spun yarn which has now become the leader.

Semi-Woollen Yarn

This is spun from a rolag with a staple length of less than 10cm (4 inches). It should be spun in a parallel direction using the short drafting technique. This

Spinning a semi-woollen yarn.

means that the drafting, twisting, and winding on is a continuous process, not like the long draw technique that is used for the woollen yarn which is an intermittent process.

Before making a semi-woollen yarn, join the leader to the bobbin and thread it the same as for the woollen yarn. Hold the leader between the thumb and first finger of your left hand, and hold the rolag three inches back from the tip between the thumb and first finger of your right hand.

Join the leader to the rolag by allowing a small amount of the fibre from the tip of the rolag to overlap the leader yarn by 2½cm (1 inch) before treadling commences (see Chapter 3 'Joining The Leader Yarn'). Your hands should be 8cm (3 inches) apart when spinning and the left hand at least 12cm (5 inches) from the orifice. When treadling, the left hand moves towards the orifice, feeding about 1 inch of yarn into the orifice, and at the same time drawing a similar length of fibre out from the rolag with the right hand to make the next inch of yarn.

As soon as the yarn has been fed in the fingers of your left hand should slip along the fibres towards the right hand, allowing the fibres to twist and make another inch of single Z yarn. Continue as above until all of the rolag has been taken up. To spin another rolag, join it as before, but to the newly spun yarn.

Wool hackle donning on/flicking.

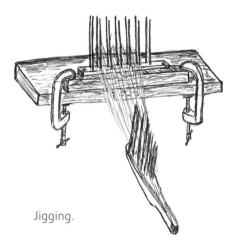

Jigging.

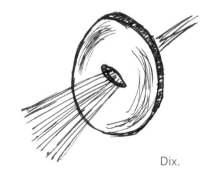

Dix.

A True Worsted Yarn

A true worsted yarn is smoother, firmer, and less hairy, with very little rough fibre protrusion. It is cooler than a woollen yarn, as the technique used when spinning a worsted yarn traps less air. Yarns spun this way do not feel as soft against the skin, but they are not prone to felting or pilling like a woollen yarn.

Not many hand spinners these days make or use a true worsted yarn as the wool combers' tools needed are not readily available, or they are very expensive. This type of yarn is spun from the fleece of the long wool or lustre group of sheep which has a staple length of at least 10cm (4 inches), or from a prepared commercial top that has been bought from a specialist craft shop.

The fibres need to be sorted into uniformity, ie quality and length, with all the double cuts and as much of the vegetation as possible removed before scouring takes place (see Chapter1 'Scouring').

Once the fibres have been washed and are completely dry, they need to be sorted by hand and laid in a flat tray. Lay the fibres tip to root in consecutive rows aligned to the yarn direction, ready to be sprayed on both sides with olive oil - 2 parts olive oil to 1 part water - using a house plant sprayer.

Combing To Make A True Worsted Yarn

Combing operates by transferring fibres from one hackle to the other. First secure the wool hackle teeth uppermost onto a worktop or table using a G-clamp. Before combing the fibres, the teeth of the hackles (combs) need to be put into a bowl of very hot water. This helps to release the oil from the fibres when combing.

✳   Start by putting the scoured wool from the tray, root first, lock by lock onto the wool hackle. This technique is called 'donning on' or flicking. Once the wool hackle is full, take the second wool hackle and, with the teeth facing down vertically, draw the wool away from the first hackle - this is known as 'jigging'. After the fibres have been transferred to the second hackle, dispose of any remaining noils (short fibres) that are on the first hackle by hand. Exchange the position of the hackles and draw off the fibres from the filled hackle into a parallel arrangement, then put them to one side. Repeat the donning on and combing out process until all the noils have been removed, leaving an arrangement consisting of only long fibres.

✳   Take the long combed fibres which are at your side, draw them through a 'dix' (a piece of leather or horn that has a hole going through the middle). This acts as an extra check for the noils.

Making A Roving

✳   After the combed fibres have gone through the dix, the fibres are laid across the palm of the left hand and held in position with the thumb. They are now drafted out with the first finger and the thumb of the right hand into a long, even strand called a roving. The thinner the strand, the thinner the yarn that can be spun. This is slightly twisted and wound onto the shaft of a drop spindle or a piece of dowelling rod.

✳   Spinning can now commence from the roving that has been wound into a ball from the shaft and has been put in to a dish on the floor, on the right hand side of the wheel. Holding the end of the roving in the left hand and the leader in the right, allow a small amount of the roving to overlap the leader as treadling begins in a clockwise direction (a Z twist). Make sure the fibres are being spun in a parallel line.

Keep the first finger and thumb of your right hand where the roving 'Vs' out from the spun yarn. Move the left hand along the roving about 2.5cm (1 inch) and hold it reasonably firmly. Move the right hand towards the left hand, preventing

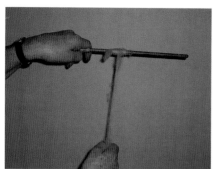

Roving being wound onto a piece of dowelling.

Spinning from a roving made from a commercial top.

any twist from passing between this hand and into the drafting zone, which lies between the two hands. Draft forward with the right hand (allowing a slight relaxation of the left hand on the fibre), and immediately move the right hand back along the drafted fibres. The twist will follow behind and a 5cm (2 inch) length of smooth yarn will be made. The left hand moves along the roving as before, while the right hand pinches the point of hold and drafts again. Repeat this process, keeping the same rhythmic movement, and also the same drafting length and the same number of twists per cm/inch along the length (see Chapter 3 'Spinning Wheels - Drive Bband And Flyer Ratios').

Worsted Type Yarn

This can be spun either straight from the fleece, which should be in very good condition, such as one that has just been shorn, with a staple length of 10cm (4 inches) or more, or by using locks that have been opened up by teasing and drawing out the fibres from both ends using fingers or a dog comb (see Chapter 4, fig 2). These fibres should be aligned in the direction of the yarn when being spun, with the tips of the locks facing the orifice, and spun using a short drafting action.

This simple method does not remove all the noils satisfactorily. Although it straightens and arranges the fibres in a parallel direction, some of the rough fibre remains, making it difficult to separate and draft the fibres while spinning to maintain a true worsted yarn. True worsted cannot be managed from fibres prepared this way, but a yarn called semi-worsted can be produced.

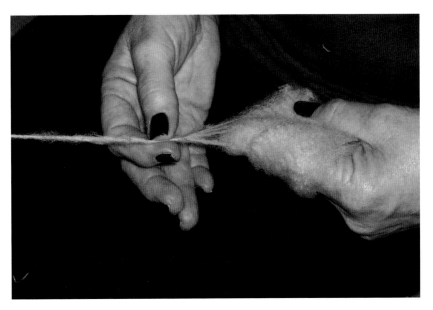

Holding the teased folded lock.

✳   A semi-worsted yarn is spun from the left hand side by first folding the teased lock over the first finger of the left hand, and holding it in position with the thumb, making sure that the lock comes right to the end of the finger tips.

✳   Before setting the wheel in motion, hold the end of the leader in the right hand and overlap a small film of the fibre onto the side of the leader (see Chapter 3 'Joining A Leader Yarn'). Set the wheel in motion in a clockwise direction (a Z twist) so a small amount of the fibre can be taken up by the leader. Keep drafting forward a small amount at a time from the V, with a short drafting movement, using the first finger and thumb of your right hand, making sure that the yarn winds onto the bobbin in a rhythmic action, and is not held back so that over twisting occurs.

✳   Repeat this process by joining the next lock to the newly spun yarn.

Joining Yarns

When joining the fibre to the newly spun yarn that has become the leader it is very important that the joins are good and cannot be noticed.

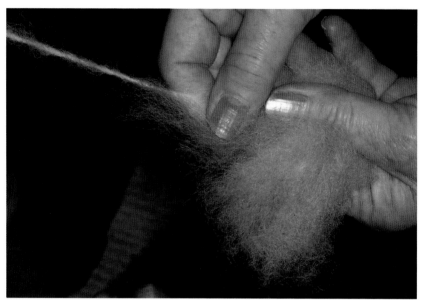

Spinning from a teased, folded lock.

If using a rolag, the fibre from the tip must overlap the leader by at least 5cm (2 inches). It should not spiral around the leader, but integrate with the leader. Hold onto the leader with your left hand, turn the drive wheel one turn with your right hand, giving the leader more twist, and draft out a small amount of the fibres from the tip of the rolag and lay them alongside the leader. The leader can now take these fibres up before commencing to spin using the long draw technique.

When spinning a true worsted or semi-worsted yarn, the fibres from the combed lock or roving should overlap the leader yarn by 2.5cm (1 inch) before spinning begins. This is so that the fibres can spiral around the leader from the side of the lock as they are spun in a parallel direction.

Basic Plying

Plying means twisting two or more threads together in the opposite direction to which the singles are spun. If the singles are spun clockwise (a Z twist), the basic plyed yarn should be spun anticlockwise (an S twist), or vice versa.

When plying the yarns they must be kept separate, either by using your fingers or by threading the singles through a piece of card or wood with holes drilled through. This is so the yarns do not get tangled, and the tension is controlled.

Three bobbins are needed when plying a basic yarn. The two full bobbins with the Z spun singles are placed on the lazy kate or bobbin rack. The third bobbin, which is empty, is put in position on the spindle of the 'U' shaped flyer to collect the yarns.

Take the two single yarns from the two bobbins and pull them through the spindle eye and orifice using the treading hook, then take both threads by hand, pass them along the bottom of the hooks of the 'U' shaped flyer to the last hook, before tying them both together onto the empty bobbin.

Before beginning to ply, the yarn is held in position with the left hand in front and the right hand behind.

Take one single yarn (A) and place it across the top of the left palm. The second single (B) is placed over the first two fingers of the left hand and then under. Both yarns are held in position with the thumb of the left hand. Take the right hand and place one single (A) over the first two fingers and under, the second single (B) goes across the right palm. These are also held in position with the thumb of the right hand .

Start plying by setting the drive wheel in motion by turning it in an anticlockwise direction to make an S twist plyed yarn, holding the double yarn straight out from the orifice with an even tension.

While plying, stop occasionally to check the yarn for the amount of twist being inserted: it is easy to make string out of two soft singles if there is too much twist. Try not to under or over twist the yarn. If the yarn is over twisting before being taken up by the bobbin, tighten the tension adjustment screw or Scotch tension, and if it is under twisting, slacken the tension (see Chapter 3 'Spinning Wheels - A Double Drive Band Wheel And Single Drive Band Wheel With A Scotch Tension).

Remember to stop more often than for spinning singles in order to move the yarn along the hooks,

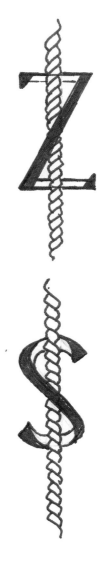

Diagram of Z and S single yarn.

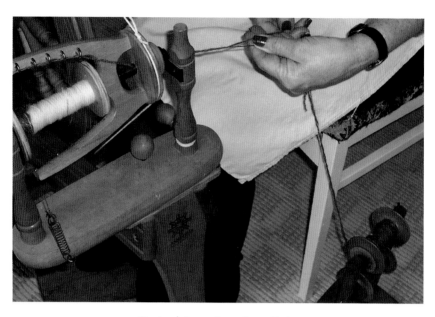

Basic plying using a Lazy Kate.

Basic plying using a shoe box

as the bobbin will fill up quicker and could overload in places. This may cause the yarn to go down between the bobbin and the 'U' shaped flyer onto the spindle, so wasting a lot of yarn.

Remember the quality of the finished plyed yarn depends on the quality of the singles, and whether they were spun tightly or loosely. The singles start to untwist a little before they start to twist together to form a plyed yarn, so if the yarn had a low degree of twist when a single yarn, the plyed yarn will be very loose, and if the single had a high degree of twist, the plyed yarn will not be so loose and you should end up with a soft and rounder thread.

When the spinning wheel does not

have either a lazy kate or a bobbin rack, it is still possible to ply the single yarns by using a cardboard box and a pair of knitting needles.

The needles are to be used as spindles, so need to be narrow enough to go through the centre of the bobbins, making sure that they can rotate freely when in situ. The box needs to be narrow enough for the knitting needles to go from one side to the other, but large enough to accommodate the two bobbins with movement when they are on the knitting needles.

Start by making two sets of holes on both sides of the box 2.5cm (1 inch) from the top, with at least 15cm (6 inches) between them. Make the hole a tight fit for the knitting needles. Take the two ends of the yarn as when plying from the lazy kate, and tie them together onto the empty bobbin, then ply as for one.

It is possible to ply a yarn from a ball of single yarn by using a commercial woolwinder. First loosen the tension adjustment screw or Scotch tension on the spinning wheel so the bobbin that is on the spindle with the single yarn runs freely. With care the yarn can now be wound onto the wool winder.

After removing the ball of single yarn from the wool winder, take the end of the yarn from the centre and the other from the edge of the ball. Holding these two ends together, put

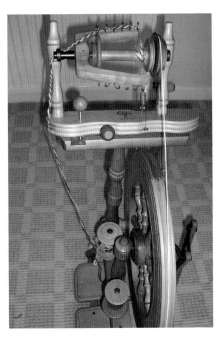

2 singles tied onto a bobbin ready for plying.

Basic plying using a bobbin rack.

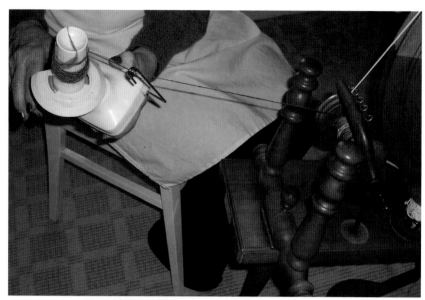

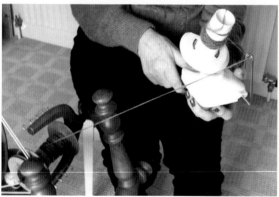

Winding a single yarn onto a commercial wool winder.

the ball of yarn into a plastic/paper bag with the threads coming through a small space at the top of the bag which has been tied with string to control the tension of the yarn. Put the bag with the yarn into a container next to the spinning wheel ready for plying. Tie the two ends of yarn onto the bobbin and ply as one. The ball of yarn will get smaller as it is plyed, so the string needs to be tied closer to the ball of yarn as it is plyed to restrict the movement of the yarn.

If a wool winder is not available, wind the wool into two single balls of yarn from the bobbin and place them in separate plastic/paper bags, as it is not possible to maintain accurate control of both the twist and ply if the balls of wool are left to run around loosely, and they will get tangled up together. Tie the yarn in the two separate bags as described above for three, making sure that the yarns have equal

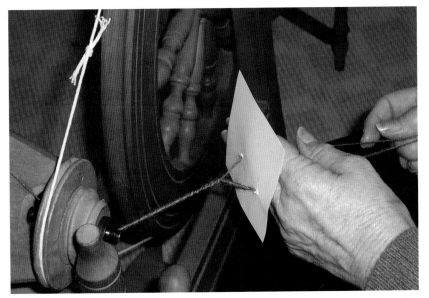

Plying from a commercially wound ball of single yarn using a piece of card to help keep the tension under control.

flow from each bag, then ply again as one.

When plying from paper bags it is a good idea to thread the yarn through a piece of wood or card as described at the beginning of the chapter.

Joining A Broken Plyed Yarn

If the single yarns should break while plying, join them back together again by taking one part of one single and laying it about 7cm (3 inches) along the side of the other part of the same single, then joining it as if using a leader yarn. Join the other single a few inches back from the join of the first. This will give a smooth, neat join which should not be noticed, especially if both yarns are the same colour. If two coloured yarns are being plyed, it is better to stop spinning if the yarn breaks and wind the plyed spun yarn into a ball, or onto the niddy noddy, then continue to ply the remaining yarn, as the join may not be as satisfactory.

Chapter 6
GETTING THE HAND SPUN YARN
READY FOR KNITTING A GARMENT

Getting The Correct Thickness

To make sure you are spinning the yarn to the correct thickness for the garment that is to be hand knitted using the commercial pattern, take a length of the commercial yarn (as a sample 3ply, 4ply double knitting etc) that has been recommended for the pattern. Put this by your side while spinning a single yarn from the fleece of your choice so that the thickness of the hand spun yarn can be compared with the commercial yarn.

After spinning about a one metre length of Z single yarn, stop and pull out part of the metre length from the bobbin. Allow this yarn to twist and fold back on itself - making it into a plyed yarn. Compare this yarn with the thickness of the commercial yarn. Once the yarn has been spun to the same, or nearly the same thickness as the commercial yarn, break off a length and tie the ends together so the single spun yarn folds and twists on itself to form a plyed yarn. Replace the commercial yarn with the hand spun yarn, and put it by your side to compare with the thickness of the yarn that is being spun.

Yarn twisting and folding back on itself.

Tension Square/Swatch

Above is just one way to get the correct thickness for knitting hand spun yarn into a garment. Another is

72

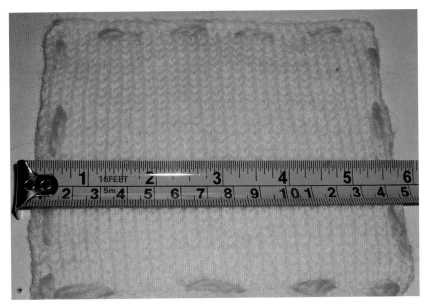

with the help of a swatch (tension square).

A pattern will only look right if knitted with the correct needles for the yarn. If in doubt, knit a few swatches with the same hand spun yarn, but with different sized knitting needles for each swatch in the stitch that is to be used for the main part of the garment.

Swatches

To know if the tension is correct, the knitted swatch should be elastic when pulled sideways. This means that when it is released it will immediately regain its original shape. If the swatch has been knitted tightly it will be stiff, the stitches will look close together, and when pulled sideways they will not stretch easily. When the swatch has been knitted loosely, the stitches will be uneven, will spread, and when pulled sideways will stretch and remain stretched. Garments knitted too tightly will lack elasticity, while garments knitted too loosely will become baggy and lose their shape.Before starting any spinning, the first priority has to be the yarn, and whether it is to be 4ply double knitting etc. Colour is also important,

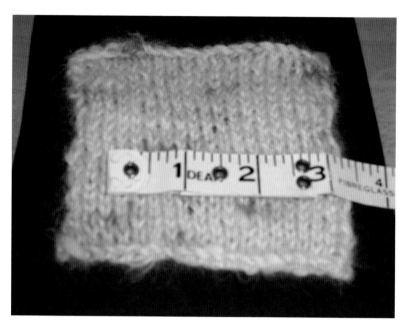

but this is the individual's choice. Some like plain and bland colours, while others like bright colours using either chemical or natural dyes. Just because at the top of the pattern it reads 'only use the wool recommended for this pattern as we cannot accept responsibility for an imperfect garment if any other brand is used', with care it is possible to change to any type of yarn you might fancy.

The first thing to do before using the knitting pattern is to knit the swatch with whichever thickness of hand spun yarn you plan to use. Any number of stitches can be used for making a swatch. If the basic knitting pattern is in stocking stitch. the same number of stitches as rows should be worked. i.e 20 stitches plus 20 rows = 1 square

If the knitting pattern has a fancy stitch for the main part, the knitter should knit a swatch in this pattern with the number of rows and stitches for the set pattern, also making sure that if the pattern has an even or odd number of stitches for each row, that these are used for both the swatch and the garment or you may get in a complete muddle, especially if using a complicated pattern.

The size of the swatch will vary with the type of wool and needles used. It should be big enough to show a few repeats of the pattern. With fine yarns a 14-15 cm (6 inch) swatch may be big enough, but when using a thicker yarn it may need to be at least a 17-18cm (7 inch) square. These dimensions will allow you to measure the number of rows and stitches per cm/inch once the swatch has been blocked, by sewing it onto a piece of card using a needle and thread. After doing this it is possible to work out how many stitches and how many rows there are per cm/inch on the swatch by using a tape measure and pinning out a 7.5cm (3 inch) square. Keep all of the swatches that have been knitted, making a note of the size of knitting needles, and the number of stitches and rows worked. They will all vary, but will come in useful at a later date for reference.

Imagine the wool recommended for the commercial pattern is double knitting and a yarn similar to an Aran has been hand spun. It will mean that fewer stitches per cm/inch will be needed as the Aran type yarn is thicker. To work out the number of stitches, first knit 2 swatches using 32 stitches with 4mm knitting needles, one with the double knitting yarn, the other with the hand spun Aran type yarn. Pin them out as I have shown above.

Once the swatches have been knitted you will need to measure across to see how many stitches there are per cm/inch. It will be noted that when using the commercial double knitting yarn with 32 stitches that there are 6 stitches per 2.5cm/1inch divide. These 6 stitches into the 32 = 14cm (5½ inches) approximately, with the Aran type yarn and using 32 stitches there are 5 stitches per 2.5cm (1 inch). Divide the 5 stitches into the 32 = 16cm (6½ inches) approximately. So the difference in the number of stitches to be used with the different yarn is 1 per cm/inch. When knitting a 40 inch (100cm) chest garment you will need to multiply 40 inches (100cm) x 5 stitches for the Aran type hand spun yarn = 200 stitches. With the commercial yarn multiply 40 inches x 6 stitches = 240 stitches. Divide both lots of stitches in half (200 = 100, 240 = 120), which means that this is the number of stitches needed for either the back or the front of the garment. This method can be used to make any size of garment.

Now the wool, knitting needle size, and the number of stitches more or less than the commercial pattern have been sorted, it is possible to knit the garment increasing or decreasing exactly as it says in your commercial knitting pattern.

When knitting a garment with hand spun yarn, a plyed yarn should be used as the finished garment will keep its shape and hang better. If the spinner decides to use a single yarn, the garment should be knitted in moss stitch, garter stitch, or rib, as these stitches may not skew, but knitting in stocking stitch with a single yarn is not a good idea as these stitches will skew, the garment will not hang correctly, and there may be difficulty when sewing the parts together as the rows may not match up, especially if blocked coloured areas have been knitted.

You could use an iron to stretch out the knitted parts of the garment. This can be done by laying the parts face down on a flat surface with pins around the edges.

Front stitches being held on a stitch holder for a side pocket.

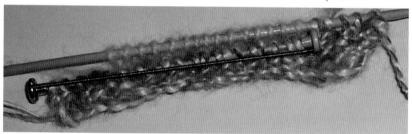

All the parts can be steam ironed by picking up and placing down the iron where needed, but do not slide the iron along the piece. A dry iron can also be used, but a damp cloth should be put on the knitted pieces before ironing commences. Care must also be taken to avoid over pressing as this may cause the garment to stretch length wise. The knitted pieces must remain stretched out until cool. Doing this will help to fix the shape of the stitches and the alignment of the garment.

It should be remembered that the fibre can be hand spun into either a woollen or a worsted yarn, but only one or the other should be used as the basic yarn for the garment. A line may appear across the hand knitting where the yarn changes from a woollen, which is heavier in weight with a medium twist and has a soft fuzzy appearance, into a worsted with a tighter twist, and a sleek and smother yarn that is lighter in weight. When the garment is washed the difference between the woollen and worsted area may be quite considerable, and it could spoil the look and the feel of the garment.

Back stitches being held on a stitch holder.

Customising A Standard Knitting Pattern

PATCH POCKETS

These can be knitted separate to the main part of the garment and added once the work is finished and has been sewn up. The pockets can either be sewn on by hand, or by using a sewing machine. If they are to go on a garment for a child they could be knitted in a contrasting fleece colour and stitched around in a different colour again. This type of pocket can be made in different shapes: square, oblong, with a V, or with a side opening; the scope is endless. They can be positioned anywhere on the garment; one near the neck and the other at the waist; it does not matter. Below are details of how I work out the positioning of a pocket accurately using graph paper.

First take a sheet of graph paper and mark the centre line from the top of the paper to the bottom. Do this by counting the number of squares across the graph paper, then halve the number (see Appendices).

It does not matter at this point how many stitches you are using for the main part of the knitting, but after marking the centre line count out the number of stitches used from this line to the side. This means that if 72 stitches are being used for the main part, halve them to 36 stitches. Now count these out from the

Grafting

centre line of the graph paper to the side. Put a ruled line from top to bottom at the 36 stitches on both sides of the middle line on the graph paper. Half the 36 stitches is 18stitches. Count in from the 36 stitch mark, and this will be the middle of the pocket. At this point put a line from top to bottom on the paper. If you wish to make a pocket for each side, mark the graph paper out the same way, but on the opposite side of the centre line.

When knitting the main part of the garment, the centre of the pocket can be marked with a length of different coloured wool. Slip the wool between stitches 18 and 19, the middle two stitches of the pocket as described on the graph. The knitter can decide how large the pocket is going to be. I would make a pocket using 26 stitches, meaning that I have added an extra 8 stitches, 4 on each side of the 18 stitches.

SQUARE PATCH POCKET

I would knit as many rows as I have stitches for this type of pocket, making it a neat square. It can be knitted in any stitch, but I recommend that it is finished off with a few rows of single rib (knit 1, purl 1).

SIDE OPENING PATCH POCKET

This can be worked the same way as for the square patch pocket using as many rows and stitches as you wish. With the front of the work facing, the first 4 stitches should be in a different stitch (single rib or single moss stitch) to the main part of the pocket, as this will be the opening to the pocket.

V PATCH POCKET

Work out the position of the pocket as I have done above. To knit the pocket cast on 4 stitches, increasing by 1 stitch at each end of every second row until 26 stitches have been picked up. Finish by knitting 4 rows in single rib, then cast off. To check if you have knitted a perfect 'V', fold the knitted piece down the middle.

SIDE POCKETS

This type of pocket is not so easy to make, as it is knitted into the main part of the garment instead of being sewn onto the main part after the garment has been completed. It is possible though, to put the pocket on either side of a jumper or a cardigan. Before beginning the pocket the knitter should consider how deep it should be, also the colour of the edging should be discussed, and whether it should blend in with the rest of the garment, or be a contrasting colour so it stands out.

With the front facing (working from the right hand side of garment), work the first 5 stitches in pattern, and pick up the next 15 stitches from the back of the next 15 stitches. Put the 15 stiches from the front row, plus the remaining stitches (30 stitches in total) onto a stitch holder.

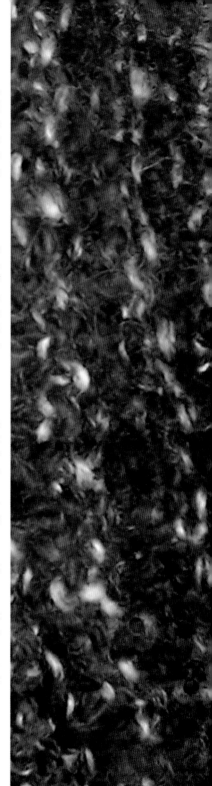

Moss stitch rib on waistcoat with crochet button holes in place.

BACK OF POCKET

Work these 15 stitches in stocking stitch, plus the 5 stitches in the main pattern (20 stitches in total) for as many rows as required for the chosen size of the pocket, but make a note of the number of rows worked. Once the back of the pocket has been worked, put these 20 stitches onto a stitch holder.

FRONT OF POCKET

Go back to the 30 stitches that are on the stitch holder at the beginning of the pocket (front facing). Knit all these stitches in the pattern, with the edge of the pocket (the first 4 stitches) being knitted in single rib - the same number of rows as for the back of the pocket will need to be worked. Then transfer all the stitches for the back of the pocket from the stitch holder onto a knitting needle with the point of the needle facing to the right hand side. With a third needle work the first 5 stitches in pattern. Return to the front of the pocket with another knitting needle, and pick up all the stitches from the stitch holder, making sure the point of this needle is also facing to the right hand side of the work

With the two needles facing in the same direction, take the third needle with the 5 stitches in place, and take one stitch from the front and one from the back row and knit them together in the pattern. For the main part continue this way until all 15 stitches have been taken up into the main part of the garment. This is called grafting with needles. Make sure that the correct number of stitches have been picked up and knitted smoothly and evenly before continuing to knit the remaining part of the garment.

RIB FOR A WAISTCOAT OR CARDIGAN

Most knitters put a single rib band (knit 1, purl 1) up the middle fronts when making either a waistcoat or a cardigan. This band is normally used for buttons/ button holes and can be as narrow or as wide as you wish, but usually 6 stitches are used. If, when the main part of the garment is finished and sewn up the garment appears tight across the chest, you can add a few more stitches when knitting the front bands: 6 stitches plus 6 more = 12 will add a little more width to the front. If the garment appears a little on the large size then simply don't add a band; just finish it off by crocheting a single chain stitch in a different colour over the first stitch of the middle fronts of the main parts, then add a crochet chain for the button holes. When doing this I normally crochet 10 chains for each button hole, making sure that I

Rib and main part sewn together.

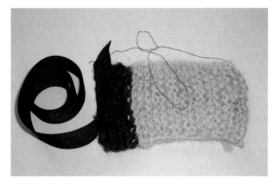

Seam binding sewn over the invisible seam.

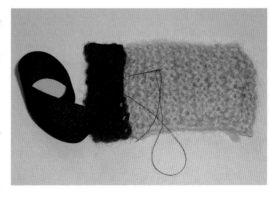

Seam binding sewn along the outside edge.

have left a long enough thread to tie the ends together, and for sewing them into the back of the main part of the knitwear. I add these before sewing on the material or seam binding.

MATERIAL OR SEAM BINDING FOR UNDER THE FRONT BORDERS

Sometimes I put a length of seam binding or material on the inside of the crocheted edge or the knitted band to stop the waistcoat or cardigan from stretching, and also to make it look more professional and tidy. Sew the knitted bands to the main part by first pinning and then tacking them in position. Take a tapestry needle with a length of woollen yarn the same colour as the main part so it blends in with the garment. Sew the parts together, making an invisible type seam. Starting at the back at the bottom front, put the needle through a stitch loop that is nearest to the edge on each side, going backwards and forwards up to the neck. Do not pull the yarn or the bands too tight as you sew, as this may cause the fronts to be of an unequal length, and consequently they may not match up.

Once the knitted bands and the main parts have been sewn together, the seam bindings are added by first tacking them in position. Do not cut them to the required length until they have been hemmed in position as you may find they are too short. Start at the bottom of the garment with a needle and some cotton thread, making sure that the outside edge is sewn first. When hemming the inside edge of the band with the binding you will notice that by sewing the outside edge first, the invisible seam is covered, making a neat edge.

When using a colourful piece of material rather than seam binding, cut the material twice as wide as required and 15cm (6 inches) longer than needed. Iron the material out on a flat surface so you are able to fold in each side and iron these folds in position, making sure the centre part is the correct width for the border. Using a sewing machine, sew down each side along the folds, and iron the material again before cutting any spare material back to the machine stitch. Stitch it in position as with the seam binding.

LENGTHENING OR SHORTENING A GARMENT

This needs to be done just before decreasing at the arm holes. If using stocking stitch, work as many cms/inches as needed. If a pattern is being knitted and it consists of a few rows, work the complete pattern set before decreasing. It is better to have a few extra rows and the garment a little longer than to get in a complete muddle when decreasing begins at the armholes.

To Add A Design To A Knitted Garment

To position a design correctly on any knitwear you will need to find a starting point which for me is the centre line on the garment. To find the centre line simply halve the number of stitches being used, ie 64 stitches halved = 32 stitches.

Then take a sheet of graph paper and find the centre line. Mark it as for the patch pocket. Count out 32 stitches from both sides of the centre line, making a line from top to bottom. This will represent the sides of the garment

The time has now come to decide on a feature. You can add anything you wish, i.e a dog, cat, snowman, flowerpot, squares, or it could be a modern design that you have drawn free hand. Do not worry if you can't draw; neither can I. Have a look at photos in magazines and if you find one you like, trace it using tracing paper and a pencil. Then transfer it over onto the graph paper. It is then the knitter's choice exactly where the feature is placed on the knitwear. In the first instance move the tracing around on the graph paper, taking note of the size of

Slip stitch colour work.

Knitted squares.

the jumper. Compare it with the size of the feature, making sure that it is not too big or too small. It is also important not to put it too near the edge, as when the knitwear is sewn up part of the feature may be sewn into the seam.

I used a single small square on the graph paper as one stitch when making the square boxes as the feature. These boxes can either be knitted in the same colour as the main part of the garment with a different stitch pattern, or by using a hand spun fancy yarn still in the same colour. A different coloured fleece can also be used, or a yarn that has been dyed with chemical or natural dye. This would mean knitting slip stitch colour work with a pattern stitch of your choice.

Slip Stitch Colour Work

This is a slip stitch that is used when changing from one colour to another to make a block of different colour when knitting a feature on a garment. When you reach the change over from brown to cream in a knit row, put a right hand needle through the next stitch, and let the brown yarn hang down the back of the knitting but over the cream yarn that will knit the next stitch, making sure that a hole does not appear. Use the same principle when working a purl row.

Mistakes When Hand Knitting

Mistakes happen for most people at one time or another while knitting. It is best to keep checking the part that is being worked from time to time as the sooner the mistake is spotted, the quicker it can be rectified. Do not be tempted to ignore the mistake as it will not go away, and you will always see it and eventually may not feel comfortable wearing the garment. Here are a few of the most common things that can go wrong

A Dropped Stitch

If the stitch has come off the needle in the middle of a row and has slipped down a few rows forming a ladder, retrieve the stitch by first getting a short length of yarn plus a crochet hook. Using the hook, pick up the stitch and slip the yarn through the stitch to stop it from slipping further down the rows. Continue to knit and work in pattern across the next row until you reach the ladder and the slipped stitch. At this point stop knitting. Using the crochet hook, take the slipped stitch up the ladder one row at a time, looping the stitch as you go and making sure that no row is missed, until you reach the row that is being worked. This is very easy to do if stocking stitch is being knitted. If it is a complicated pattern you should perhaps think again. It may be easier after saving the stitch with the yarn to undo the rows down to the slipped stitch and start knitting up from there. If the row that has been reached is not the beginning of the set pattern you might also need to undo a few extra rows before starting to knit them up again.

Neck Too Tight On A Child's Jumper

It is very difficult to judge the size the neck will need to be, and once you have knitted up the neck it is very disheartening to find it is far too tight to go over the head of the child for whom it is intended.

Before knitting up the neck, sew the front and back of the right shoulders together. Do not sew up across the left shoulder but pick up the correct number of stitches evenly across this shoulder. If you cast off 15 stitches across the left shoulder when finishing the main part of the jumper that is the number that will need to be picked up. Pick up these stitches across the front of the left shoulder and knit 4 rows in single rib cast off. Do the same for the back of the left shoulder. Put 3 poppers evenly along the ribbed stitches to join the opening. When picking up the stitches to knit the neck, do remember to pick up 4 extra stitches on both sides of the opening.

Round Neck Band

It is sometimes difficult to get the correct number of stitches for the neck band, and when a jumper and the neck band are completely finished you may notice that the neck is slightly askew.

In the first instance it is very important to make sure that the correct number of stitches have been picked up on both sides of the neck. It does not matter if more or less rows are knitted than what is specified in the pattern, but the sides should be even in the number of stitches.

Sew up the right side shoulder, and with the front facing pick up the stitches evenly down the left side (making a note of the number picked up). Pick up the stitches from a safety pin placed across the bottom of the neck. Pick the stitches up on the right hand side again, making a note of the number, and then the stitches across the back of the neck (which should be the same number cast off for the back of the main part of the garment).

Subtract the number of stitches on the left hand side from the number on the right or vice versa. Whichever side has the least number of stitches should have the extra stitches added evenly along that particular side, eg if there are 24 stitches already down one side and 4 more stitches are needed, divide the 4 into 24 = 6, so add one extra stitch after every 6 stitches worked.

Joining A Yarn

When knitting, a new yarn should be joined at the beginning of the row and not in the middle. You should start using the yarn 8cm (3 inches) in from the end, leaving enough to be sewn in along the back of the knitting once it is finished. Remember not to knot and cut the ends as this makes the back of the work very untidy.

If the yarn is joined with a knot in the middle of the row it could show through to the front of the knitting, or if two lengths of yarn are left hanging in the middle, a hole could appear thus spoiling the effect. If you have to join the yarn in the middle of the row due to lack of yarn you can always twist the 2 yarns around one another once, making sure they are facing in opposite directions before slipping the yarns along the stitches at the back of the work while knitting.

Square Hat With A Rolled Brim

This pattern is very easy to knit and an ideal introduction for anyone knitting with hand spun yarn for the first time. You can use any type of stitch but I recommend single moss stitch, as the yarn could be over twisted in parts, especially if you are a beginner to hand spinning. If knitting the hat in stocking stitch you may notice skewed stitches, but if using single moss stitch the skew may not be quite as visible to the eye.

Moss stitch: *1st row = knit 1, purl 1 to the end of the row*
                 2nd row = purl 1, pnit 1 to the end of the row

   These 2 rows form the pattern

Using yarn that has been hand spun similar to 4 ply or double knitting:

• Cast on 90 stitches with size 3 3/4mm (9) needles and work 7cm (3 inches)
• Change to size 4mm (8) needles and work straight until 30cm (12 inches) from the beginning has been knitted. Cast off, turn the work inside out, and sew up the side seam and the cast off edge with an invisible stitch.

With the hat the right way you will notice at the top of the hat that the corners are pointed. Take the 2 corners and fold them, one at a time, so that the points meet in the middle at the top of the hat. Sew the points together in the centre then add a button, or perhaps you might prefer to plait some spun yarn then sew one plait on each corner and tie them together in a bow in the centre. I sometimes fold the corners down at the sides of the hat and sew them in position. I then add buttons, one on each side. You will perhaps notice that on the hat I have made I have folded the corners up onto the sides of the top and added ceramic buttons.

Chapter 7

DIFFERENT TYPES OF FANCY HAND SPUN YARN

Some people think of hand spun yarn as flawed, irregular, and rough. This is actually a very sad misconception as these days it is by no means a necessity to spin your own yarn, but more a luxury as the equipment and fibres etc are quite expensive and the process rather time consuming.

Designing different types of yarn involves fibre preparation before hand spinning with either a spindle or a spinning wheel. The outcome of the yarn should not occur by chance but as the result of a controlled preparation. With practice you should be able to design a perfect yarn similar to any that can be bought from the local wool shop.

As well as using wool for fancy yarns it is also possible to use different fibres such as alpaca, mohair, angora, silk, soya protein fibre, and bamboo, to name just a few. All these fibres need to be spun with a certain amount of wool, especially if the yarns are to be used for knitting. The reason for this is because these fibres on their own may not bounce back into shape when washed, and when made into a garment they could just hang with no 'spring'. When I spin any of these fibres into a yarn I use 50/50 - 1 bobbin with wool and 1 bobbin with a different fibre.

As the mohair and the angora are very fluffy, it is difficult to make a complete yarn, and is best to add them over the top of a fine spun yarn while it is being plyed. This will give the yarn a very soft feel. A small amount can be added to the wool while it is being carded by laying whichever fibre is required over the top of the wool when it is on a hand carder or the drum carder. Remember to lay the fibre in the same direction as the wool locks.

Silk, bamboo, and soya protein fibre can all be spun into a yarn if a single yarn

Single yarn carded and spun using 2 colours.

of wool is used with each of them. Another option is to take a lock of teased wool with a lock of commercial fibre and align them next to each other (see Chapter 'Spinning A Lock'), alternating them as they are being spun, i.e wool, fibre and so on.

These different fibres are available from specialist craft shops and can be bought on the Internet.

When spinning fancy yarns, woollen, semi-worsted, or a true worsted yarn may be spun for the basic yarn; it is the spinner's own choice unless it has been stated otherwise. The basic yarns below have all been spun using wool that has been made into a semi-worsted yarn.

Single Yarn

• This is a yarn that has been spun in a Z twist with one colour, or with two colours lined up together. This means that fleece with the same length staple has been combed or carded with the two colours lying side by side.

Basic Even Plyed Yarn

• Fill 2 bobbins with Z twist single yarns, both with the same colour or with two different colour yarns, i.e one bobbin filled with cream and the other with brown. Put the 2 full bobbins with the Z twist singles on either the lazy kate or the bobbin rack and ply the 2 yarns together in an S twist. The two yarns should be held with equal tension, as if they are not then the slacker of the two may spiral around the tensioned yarn, making the plyed yarn irregular.

• A yarn that has been plyed with an irregular tension will be noticeable when knitted as the stitches will be sloping, especially if they are knitted in stocking stitch When the garment is completed you may see a few rows of stitches on the slope in one area which may spoil the effect of the whole garment, especially if it is in a prominent position.

Spiral Yarn Using Black Welsh Mountain Fleece With Chemically Dyed Silk

- Fill the first bobbin with a medium firmly twisted Z single yarn (Black Welsh Mountain).

- Fill the second bobbin with a fine firmly twisted Z single yarn. This will be used as the core (dyed silk).

- To ply, allow the fine yarn (the core yarn) to go into the orifice first and tie this yarn onto the bobbin, then allow the thicker single yarn to wrap around the thin yarn, while the thin yarn is held at a 45 degree angle and kept taut.

- To do this the spinning wheel is turning in an anticlockwise direction, making an S twist. Do not be tempted to hold the medium yarn loosely as this will produce a yarn that will slide along the core. You may need to loosen the drive band so as to make a slower delivery of the twist. Handle the completed yarn with care as the medium yarn may move along the core yarn.

Knob Yarn Using Black Welsh Mountain And Merino Fleece

- Fill 2 bobbins with 2 different coloured Z single yarns.

- Ply the 2 yarns together in an S twist. Use the yarn intended to be decorated as as the core. Whichever one this is will be the choice entirely of the spinner. The other yarn needs to be twisted around the core

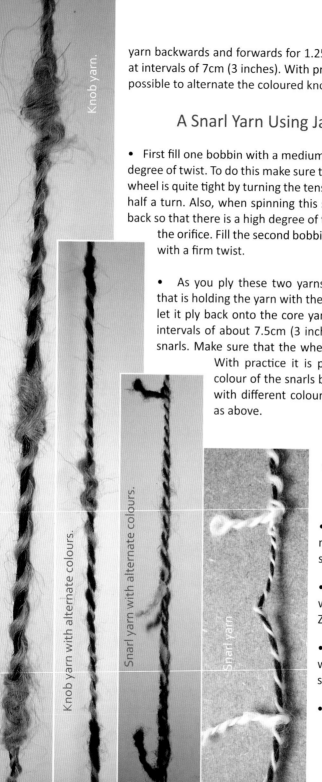

Knob yarn.

Knob yarn with alternate colours.

Snarl yarn with alternate colours.

Snarl yarn

Snarl yarn

yarn backwards and forwards for 1.25cm (½ inch) 3 or 4 times at intervals of 7cm (3 inches). With practice it will also become possible to alternate the coloured knobs.

A Snarl Yarn Using Jacob Fleece

• First fill one bobbin with a medium Z single yarn with a high degree of twist. To do this make sure that the drive band on the wheel is quite tight by turning the tension adjustment screw up half a turn. Also, when spinning this single yarn hold the yarn back so that there is a high degree of twist while feeding it into the orifice. Fill the second bobbin with a fine Z single yarn with a firm twist.

• As you ply these two yarns S twist, relax the hand that is holding the yarn with the high degree of twist and let it ply back onto the core yarn for 1.25cm (½ inch) at intervals of about 7.5cm (3 inches). This will make little snarls. Make sure that the wheel is turning very slowly. With practice it is possible to alternate the colour of the snarls by first filling the bobbins with different coloured yarn and then plying as above.

Gimp Yarn Using Wensleydale And Jacob Fleece

• Fill one bobbin with a medium firmly twisted Z single yarn.

• Fill the second bobbin with a fine firmly twisted Z single yarn.

• Fill the third bobbin with a fine twisted S single yarn.

• Ply the first and second

bobbin together in an S twist direction, allowing the medium yarn to spiral around the fine yarn to make a 2 ply yarn.

• Ply the 2 plyed yarn with the third bobbin in a Z twist direction. It may help if you hold the third yarn at a 45 degree angle. When spinning this yarn there must be a big difference between the medium and fine yarns so that the fine waves are noticeable.

Single Marl Yarn

• This is a Z single yarn spun from two rovings of different colours placed side by side before being spun.

Double Marl Yarn

• Fill two bobbins with Z single marl yarn as shown above, choosing either four different shades of fleece, or two shades of fleece on one bobbin with two different colours of naturally dyed fleece on the other, making two colours on each bobbin. This means that when the two yarns have been S plyed, the yarn will have four colours running through it, making a four colour yarn.

Half Marl Yarn

• Fill one bobbin with a Z single yarn of your choice.

• The second bobbin should be filled with Z single marl yarn.

• S ply the two yarns together to make a three colour yarn.

Slub Yarn

• Fill two bobbins with single Z twist yarn. The yarns can be of the same colour or differing colours.

Gimb yarn.

Single marl yarn.

93

Double marl yarn.

Half Marl Yarn.

- S ply them together, adding a different colour over the top at 5cm (2 inch) intervals. It is possible to add more than one colour by holding small amounts of different coloured fleece in the palm of the right hand and alternating the colours while treadling very slowly when S plying.

Add colour to a rolag by carding different coloured fleece together with natural or chemically dyed fleece. Make sure the locks are all the same length and facing in the same direction, either root or tip first but not a mixture when laying the brown, grey and then cream fleece across the carder.

- Add tiny amounts of the dyed fleece at intervals over the top of the natural coloured fleece. Make quite a few rolags this way when they are spun together as below, and a wonderful tweed effect will appear.

- Fill two bobbins of Z single yarns.

- S ply the two yarns together.

Textured Yarn

A simple textured yarn can be made by filling two bobbins with Z spun singles, one being filled with thick yarn and the other with a thin yarn. When plying these yarns together, hold one with greater tension than the other (this being the core yarn, with the slacker tensioned yarn spiralled around it). The tension can be reversed at intervals along the yarn .

Coloured rolags with carder.

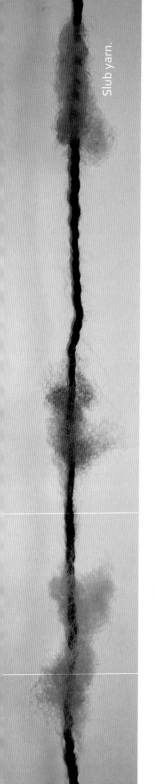

Slub yarn.

Plyed Spun Yarn.

Textured yarn.

The natural dyes that I use come from the plants that I am able to collect from the hedgerows when I am out walking, or from the plants that have grown in my own garden. I enjoy watching the tiniest of seeds that have been sown in my greenhouse as they start to shoot, and when transferred, grow into mature plants in my flower borders, ready to use for dyeing my fleeces.

Most plants grown will yield a colour but they are not all fast. The easiest colours to obtain are yellows, browns, and fawns. There are a few blues and reds, with even fewer greens.

Before starting any mordanting or natural dyeing, the fleece or yarn will need to be scoured, and all the dirt and natural grease removed, as leaving any of the grease in will result in uneven dyeing (see Chapter 1 'Scouring A Fleece'). Wool can be dyed direct from the scoured fleece, or after it has been spun into a yarn and made into a skein and scoured. Tie the skein loosely in a few places. Skeins that are tied too tightly will have undyed patches beneath the ties. The ties help to keep the yarn in order and prevent it from tangling when in the dye bath. Use string for this purpose as this will be easily identified when it needs to be removed.

Fleece from different types of sheep may give a different colour, even when the same mordant and dye stuff has been used. When dyeing still think of the quality of the wool; a coarse wool may pick up the colour better than a soft wool, or vice versa.

The amount of water that is put in the saucepan does not need to be exact but

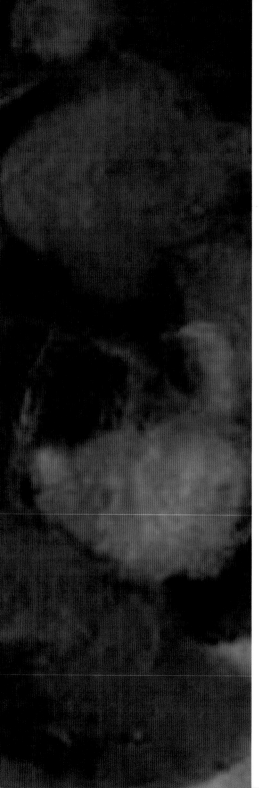

there should be enough to cover the wool and dye stuff to allow freedom of movement for both. Do not put dry wool into the dye or mordant bath; it must be wet and should be added to the mordant bath after the mordant has been stirred into the water and completely dissolved or you may get uneven colours.

Tap water plays an important part in the dyeing process, the hardness or softness of the water determining to some extent the colours you will get. If you are given a dye recipe from a friend in the next town or village who has soft water, the colour from the recipe may be red, but you may get a different colour from the same recipe, due to the fact that your water is hard.

When reading books on natural dyeing you will notice that they do not agree on some of the colours and quality of dye you will get from certain plants. Some plants actually vary from year to year due to the chemical substances that they contain.

It is important to identify the plants accurately, and this too can be difficult at times as there are quite a few varieties of brambles, dandelions, roses etc, and all may give a different dye colour. Using the common name rather than the latin name does not help as the common name may vary from district to district, and from country to country.

Great pleasure can be gained from collecting and using dye stuff from

plants in the hedgerow, but always ensure you take only a minimum from each plant rather than denuding any one plant completely. Leave enough flower heads on each plant to provide seed for a plant to grow again the following year.

Try to pick enough dye stuff in one go, as the plants can sometimes be affected by the weather and soil conditions, so that when you return to collect some more you may find that the conditions have changed, and when boiling up the dye stuff a different colour may appear, even though you boiled it up exactly the same as before. Remember not to dig up any roots as this will destroy the plant, and it is illegal to dig up roots from the countryside.

Mordants

Most plants used for natural dyeing need a fixing agent - this is known as a mordant and it chemically fixes the dye to the wool, helping to make the dye fast so the colour stays in the fibre. When using a different mordant with the same dye stuff it can change the colour of the fibre.

It is possible to mordant wool before dyeing, during dyeing, or even after the wool has been in the dye bath.

Before Dyeing...

Mix the mordant with a little water in an old cup until dissolved, then add the

GARDEN

BLACKBERRY DYE

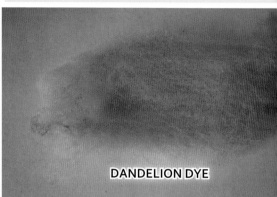

DANDELION DYE

ELDERBERRY DYE

DOCK LEAF DYE

IVY BERRY DYE

LETTUCE DYE

DYES

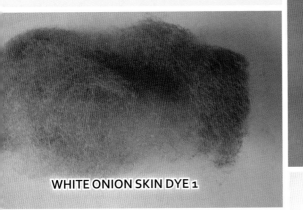

WHITE ONION SKIN DYE 1

WHITE ONION SKIN DYE 2

RED ONION SKIN DYE

RHUBARB LEAF DYE 1

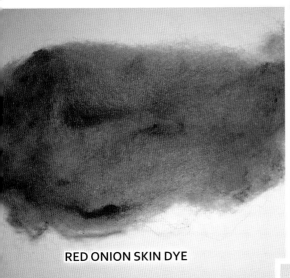

ROSE PETAL /DAFFODIL DYE

RHUBARB LEAF DYE 2

Part of my dyeing shed.

mordant mixture to the water in the mordanting saucepan, stirring well with a length of dowelling rod. Always make sure that there is enough water to cover the wet wool and dye stuff. Add the wool and the chosen dye stuff tied up in a muslin and heat up the saucepan. Better results occur this way, ie brighter colours.

During Dyeing...

Mix the mordant as above and put it into the saucepan of water, stirring well. After cutting up the dye stuff very small and tying it in muslin, add it to the saucepan of cold water. Now put the wet wool into the pan, again confirming that there is enough water for the free movement of both dye stuff and wool.

After Dyeing...

Cut up the dye stuff as before and tie it in the muslin. Add this with the wet, scoured wool to the water in the dye bath. Heat it up as before, allowing the water to cool naturally before removing the wet wool and adding it to the mordant pan, then heating it up again. It is possible to do this with any dye stuff.

If iron (ferrous sulphate) is used as the mordant it is important to remove the wool from the dye bath 30 minutes before finishing the dyeing. After removing the wool, add the mixed mordant to the water in the dye bath and stir well, before returning the wool to finish the dyeing process with the mordant.

Alum is the most commonly used mordant, but some of the others are not easy to obtain and must be ordered from specialist shops (see 'Suppliers').

Alum - potassium aluminium sulphate is a very popular mordant and is used with cream of tartar. This helps to brighten the colour and keep the wool soft, but using too much alum will make the wool sticky.

Chrome - bichromate of potash (poisonous orange crystals) should be stored in dark bottles as the crystals are sensitive to light. It is very good to use if orange and red colours are needed. These colours can be obtained by using onion skins, madder, or brazil wood as the dye stuff.

Copper sulphate (poisonous blue crystals) will give differing shades of bronze when using as a mordant with dock or sorrel plants. If using elder leaves or lettuce plants (Fortune lettuce that has gone to seed) it is possible to obtain a deep green.

Iron - ferrous sulphate (green crystals) tends to sadden colours and has a hardening effect on the fibres.

Tin - stannous chloride (white crystals) gives a bright colour when used as a mordant with most dye stuffs, and only a small amount is required. Too much will, however, make the wool brittle.

Cream of tartar - potassium bitartrate is an acid salt that is usually used in cooking and wine making. It can be used to modify the hardening effects of some of the mordants, ie ferrous sulphate, alum and tin. It also helps to brighten the colours, as well as helping the mordant to attach to the wool.

Equipment

Use a stainless steel, oven proof glass, or enamel saucepan (but if the enamel is chipped, any rust will affect the colour of the wool) for boiling up both dye stuff and mordants. If you are using alum as a mordant, an aluminium saucepan can be used, but do NOT use this pan as a dye bath as the aluminium may affect the colour of the wool.

I find it best to have one saucepan for the dye stuff and a different one for the mordants, and the larger the saucepans used, the better. If space is available it is a good idea to have enough saucepans for all the different mordants you are likely to use as the chemicals will eventually affect the saucepan and the colour of the wool, especially if all the different mordants are being used in the same

pan. It is a good idea to put a label on the saucepans with the name of the mordant or dye being used in those particular pans.

A notepad and pen are important for recording the time of year for picking the dye stuff, which mordant was used, and for how long the wool was simmered in the mordant and dye bath.

I recommend that rubber gloves are worn when mordanting, as some mordants irritate the skin while others may stain the hands. An apron too should be worn in case of any spillage, with a dust mask over the nose and mouth to stop any fumes being inhaled.

You should also have to hand scissors for cutting up the dye stuff, string and muslin for making dye bags, a timer, a set of small scales for weighing the mordants, and larger scales for weighing the wool and dye stuff. Non-metallic spoons will also be needed for measuring the chemicals, and a length of dowel rod for stirring the baths.

For the mordants and dyeing wool should not be used for any other purpose and should be kept well away from children. Most of the mordants are poisons, so should be kept in a special box in either a locked cupboard or store room where all the other equipment is kept.

If the dyeing has to be done in the kitchen and not in a specially designed shed, make sure that you are not doing it while you are cooking or have food around, and also make sure that whereever the dyeing and mordanting is done that windows can be opened to release any fumes that will occur.

PROBLEMS THAT CAN OCCUR WHILE DYEING

The colour will not fix to the wool.	The reason is usually that the wool has not been scoured properly and grease and soap flakes are still present. The wool has not been in the mordant or dye bath for long enough.
The colour comes off the wool and onto your hands, even though the wool is dry.	The wool has not been scoured correctly, and grease is still in situ. The dye stuff has not been rinsed out of the wool properly.
The wool felts.	The wool has been stirred while in the dye or mordant bath. The wool has had a sudden change of temperature. If the wool is put into a pan with cold water and is slowly taken up to near boiling it will not felt. It will only felt if put straight into very hot water. If the saucepan is not big enough for the amount of wool being used, this will mean that the wool at the bottom of the pan will get hotter than the wool at the top, so it may felt.
Uneven dyeing.	Tying the skeins too tightly. Too much wool in too small a pan, so there is not enough room for the wool, the dye, and the water. Grease left in the fleece or skein after scouring.
Saucepans.	Make sure they are washed thoroughly with wire wool between each use. Do not just rinse and leave any washing up liquid in the pan as this may affect the colour when a particular pan is used again.

TEA BAG DYE

NATURAL

GROUND COFFEE DYE

BRAZIL WOOD DYE

MADDER 1

MADDER 2

DYES

MADDER DYE 3

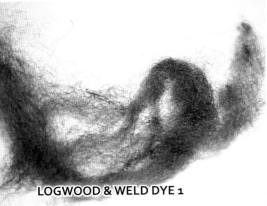

LOGWOOD & WELD DYE 1

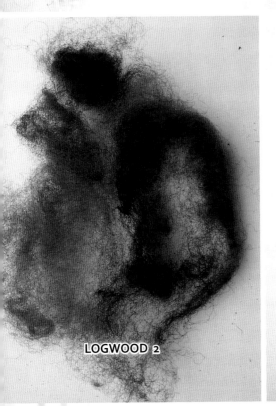

LOGWOOD 2

LOGWOOD 3

Recipes

These recipes are very easy to use, and the plants should be easy to find, either in your garden or the hedgerow. I have used 250g (8 oz) of wool for each recipe, unless otherwise stated. Hard water has been used with all of these recipes.

Hard dye stuff (bark, twigs and roots) needs to be chopped up small, and may need to be boiled for longer periods, ie 2 hours to extract the colour. It helps to soften these dye stuffs by covering them with boiling water and leaving them to soak overnight before boiling them up altogether the next morning. Onion skins, flower heads, soft berries, and leaves (soft dye stuffs), need a shorter boiling period, ie up to one hour, and will not need to soak overnight.

It must be remembered that the wool will not felt if the water is taken from cold to nearly boiling with the wool in situ. It will only felt if it is put straight into very hot water.

WILD BLACKBERRIES
250g wild blackberries
125g fustic chips
½ tsp stannous chloride
½ tsp cream of tartar

DANDELION HEADS (TARAXACUM OFFICINALE)
(for 100g wool)
250g dandelion heads
1 tsp chrome (bichromate of potash)
A few drops of formic acid

DOCK LEAF PLANT (GRANNY'S SUMMER FIRST AID KIT)
(for 100g wool)
250g dock leaves cut up very small
1 tsp chrome (bichromate of potash)
½ tsp copper sulphate
½ tsp cream of tartar

ELDERBERRIES
½ tsp chrome (bichromate of potash)
A few drops formic acid

RIPE IVY BERRIES
1 tsp chrome (bichromate of potash)
½ tsp folic acid
½ tsp cream of tartar

LETTUCE
(I recommend Fortune lettuce that has gone to seed)
Lettuce chopped up very small
½ tsp iron sulphate
1 tsp cream of tartar

WHITE ONION SKINS - *Recipe #1*
250g white onion skins
½ tsp chrome (bichromate of potash)
A few drops of formic acid

WHITE ONION SKINS - *Recipe #2*
250g white onion skins
½ tsp tin (stannous chloride)
½ tsp oxalic acid (or 5cm (2 inches) rhubarb stalk from near the ground)
1 tsp cream of tartar

ONION SKINS (RED)
250g red onion skins
½ tsp tin (stannous chloride)
½ tsp cream of tartar

RHUBARB LEAVES - *Recipe #1*
250g rhubarb leaves cut up small
½ tsp tin (stannous chloride)
1 tsp cream of tartar

RHUBARB LEAVES - *Recipe #2*
250g rhubarb leaves cut up small
½ tsp tin (stannous chloride)
½ tsp copper sulphate
1 tsp cream of tartar

ROSE PETALS OR DAFFODIL HEADS
250g rose petals or daffodil heads
½ tsp chrome (bichromate of potash)
A few drops of formic acid
½ tsp cream of tartar

Many dried herbs are found in the back of kitchen larders, having been bought for use with a particular food recipe, and sometimes there they have remained, unused until they are out of date. Before throwing them out, boil them up with a little wool. I think you will be pleasantly surprised as older herbs give a better colour than many fresh from the garden. You can dye the wool without a mordant, but the colour may not be as vivid and it may fade with time.

Below are just a few of the kitchen larder items that can be used. I suggest in the first instance that you use anything for dyeing wool that is on its way to the dustbin from the kitchen larder, as this may start you out on the exciting road to colour preparation.

Curry powder

Gold or cream colours can be obtained, but the colour is usually not very bright.

Turmeric

This is a yellow powder for colouring foods. It comes from ground up tubers (*Curcuma longa* or *Curcuma tinctoria*) that have been grown in India and China. The dye is substantive and is very popular with novice dyers. Many of us have this in the larder, but if you have not got any, go to any supermarket - it is relatively cheap. It will give a yellow colour using the tiniest amount of stannous chloride as the mordant.

Used Tea Bags

Save them until you have enough; twenty or so will do. The colour will be an amazing yellow without a mordant. I use Tesco tea bags, but if you use another make you may get a different colour. Try it!

Coffee

Using the dregs from the ground coffee beans I have been known to get a brown shade without the use of a mordant.

Dye Stuff That I Buy In

I buy some of my dye stuff from craft shops (see 'Suppliers'). I use these in the same way that I use my garden and hedgerow plants, unless otherwise stated.

Fustic chips

From the heartwood of the Mactura Tinctoria tree, they are commonly known as dyers' Mulberry. It is a medium to large American tropical tree. Fustic yeilds a range of yellow colours and has a good light fastness. It is a very good dye for mixing with other dye stuff.

Fustic chips	with	**LOGWOOD and bio chromate**	Green/Yellow
"	" with	**WOAD**	Bright green
"	" with	**COPPER SULPHATE**	Olive green
"	" with	**FERROUS SULPHATE**	Dark green
"	" with	**STANNOUS CHLORIDE and cream of tartar**	Bright yellow

BRAZIL WOOD TREE (CAESALPINIA ECHINATA))

Portuguese explorers found this growing on the coast of South America in the late 1500s. The dye comes from the heart of the tree and yields a rich red colour. These days it can be sourced and imported commercially from Asia.

250g Brazil wood chips or saw dust
1 tsp chrome (bichromate of potash)
A few drops of Formic acid

This dye bath can be used several times, but each time a paler colour will be achieved.

MADDER (RUBIA TINCTORUM)

This is an evergreen perennial plant that is native to the Mediterraen and Southern Europe. All parts of the madder plant contains the anthraquinone pigment alizarin which makes the red dye, but the root has the highest concentration. This plant matures in 5 years, and this is the time to take the dye stuff. The dye bath can be reused several times but each time a paler colour will occur. The madder root needs to be tied in muslin and soaked over night in the saucepan that is to be used as the dye bath (use 125gr of madder root for each recipe).

Recipe #1
125g madder root
½ tsp tin (stannous chloride)
½ tsp oxalic acid (or 5cm (2 inches) rhubarb stalk from near the ground)
½ tsp cream of tartar

Recipe #2
125g madder root
1tsp alum (potassium aluminium sulphate)
1 tsp cream of tartar Fig 2

Recipe #3
Madder root (125gr)
1 teaspoonful of chrome (bichromate of potash)
2 tsp formic acid

WELD PLANT

This can be found growing wild in the English countryside.

LOGWOOD TREE (HAEMATOXYLUM CAMPECHIANUM)

The logwood tree grows in Central America, and the dye comes from the heartwood of the tree. It is exported as wood chip.

Recipe #1
125g each of logwood chips and weld
½ tsp chrome (bichromate of potash)
A few drops of formic acid

Recipe #2
125g logwood chips
½ tsp chrome (bichromate of potash)
A few drops of formic acid

Recipe #3
125g logwood chips
½ tsp oxalic acid (or 5cm (2 inches) rhubarb stalk from near the ground)
½ tsp tin (stannous chloride)
H½ tsp cream of tartar

Basic Details For Mordanting And Dyeing Wool

Take the saucepan which is to be used for the mordant and put a label on the side with the name of the mordant being used. Fill the pan with cold water, then add the mordant (already dissolved in a little water) to the pan. Stir it well using a length of dowelling rod.

Add the scoured, wet wool (250g (8oz) to the specified recipe ingredients, unless otherwise stated) to the mordanting pan, making sure that there is enough water for free movement of the amount of wool being used. Slowly bring the water containing the wool up to close to boiling point, and simmer for 45 minutes without stirring as this may cause the wool to felt and dye unevenly. Halfway through the mordanting process turn the wool over once very carefully using a pair of tongs, so that the wool at the bottom of the pan is moved to the top. If it is not turned over the wool at the bottom may become felted, as the water at the bottom of the pan is considerably hotter than that at the top.

After forty five minutes take the pan off the stove with the wool still in situ, and leave it to cool naturally in the open air. This will give the wool more time to absorb the mordant, and also make it cooler, safer and easier to handle when removing the wool from the pan with the tongs. Let the wool drain before rinsing in warm water, then squeeze it gently. Do not ring it out. Keep the mordanted wool in a bucket of clean water if it is not going to be used straight away for dyeing. The mordanted wool is now ready to use.

Before disposing of the mordanted water down the sink, it must be remembered that this water is poisonous and that there are restrictions on substances that can enter the sewer. First consult your local water authority, who will discuss with you the best way to dispose of the mordanted water.

Take the other pan and label it with the name of the dye stuff that is to be used. Fill the it with cold water, and take the dye stuff, ie onion skins, and chop them up using a pair of scissors. Put them into muslin with enough material for the free movement of the onion skins, and tie it up tightly with string. Now the dye stuff can go into the pan with the cold water. Bring the saucepan slowly up to boiling point, stirring and prodding with the dowelling rod to extract the colour. Boil it with care for forty five minutes, then take the pan off the stove and leave it with the water and dye stuff still in situ to cool naturally in the open air.

Once the dye bath has cooled, the damp pre-mordanted wool can be put into the dye bath, making sure the wool is completely covered by the water and the pan is large enough to accommodate all the wool and dye stuff with free movement. The dye stuff can be removed before heating up the wool in the pan if you wish, or it can remain in the water. I usually leave it in.

Bring the dye bath with the wool slowly up to nearly boiling point and simmer for forty five minutes. Do not stir the wool but turn it over once, as when mordanting. After forty five minutes remove the pan from the stove and leave it with the water and wool still in situ to cool naturally. Once the water has cooled, take the dyed wool out of the pan and rinse it in warm, soapy water. Allow the wool to dry in the open air but in the shade as heat from direct sunlight may affect the wool and the colour.

When you dye 'in the fleece' and it is laid out to dry, you will find that the top of the fibre may be several degrees lighter than the layers beneath, so when the fibre is spun into yarn many shades of one colour will show up in the yarn. Natural dyes are enhanced by age and will mellow into a natural beauty.

After dyeing the wool with natural dyes there is usually some dye residue left in the dye bath (this is called exhaust), making it possible to dye another amount of wool. The colour, however, will be lighter than the first and may not be as fast.

Random Dyed Yarn

This means the yarn has more than one colour running through the different areas of the skein.

To do this first make a skein of basic plyed yarn using a cream fleece. Scour this yarn, making sure all of the grease is removed. Place the skein in a mordant bath using a mordant of your choice, and heat it up as shown before. Leave it to cool naturally then remove the wool from the pan, rinsing it to remove excess mordant. You will need 2 different dye baths for the pre-mordanted yarn.

Once the skein has completely dried, wet one end. Place the dye bath on the stove and, exercising care, hang the skein of pre-mordanted yarn above the dye bath, low enough for the wet end of the skein to enter into the bath. Heat up the dye bath with the skein in this position, and simmer for forty five minutes, then leave the bath to cool with the yarn still in this position. Remove the skein from the dye bath after it has cooled, and rinse the yarn.

To be safe, dry all of the skein completely in the shade before dyeing the other end. Wet the undyed end thoroughly and tie it up again above the second dye pan with the undyed end in the pan. Heat it up again as before.

GLOSSARY OF TERMS

Alpaca Animal related to a llama which produces alpaca fibre

Angora goat Animal that produces mohair

Angora rabbit Long haired rabbit that produces angora fibre

Ashford A make of spinning wheel

Batt Another name for a sliver

Bobbin The reel that is put on the spindle for the yarn to be spun onto.

B.W.M.B British Wool Marketing Board

Britch Coarse fleece

Carding Preparing a fibre to spin a woollen yarn

Count Quality of wool

Combing A lock ready for spinning a worsted yarn

Crimp The natural kink in the lock of a fleece

Diamond Part of the fleece with a shorter staple which is lacking in oil

Donning on Adding locks to a wool hackle

Double cuts Tiny nips of wool caused by the shearer making a second pass while shearing. They are found on the under side of the fleece

Drafting Pulling the fibres out between the fingers

Exhaust Weaker colour

Extra Diamond Finer and greasier part of the fleece

Flyer 'U' shaped attachment with the spindle that holds the bobbin in position on the spinning wheel

Foot-man Moves up and down and is linked to the drive wheel via the crank at the top and the treadle cord at the bottom. It is this that operates the main drive wheel

Great wheel Another name for the walking wheel

Handle The feel of the fleece

Hog Fleece from a first shearing

'In the Grease' Spinning from a fleece that has not been scoured

Jigging Transfering locks from one hackle to another

Kemp Thick, hairy fibre

Leader yarn The spinner attaches the fibre to the leader at the start of any spinning

Lock Fibres from a fleece root to tip

Lazy Kate A rack for placing the bobbins when plying the singles

Maidens The uprights that holds the 'U' shaped flyer in position

Mother of all Part of the spinning wheel that carries the maidens

Mohair Fibre from an angora goat

Mordants Chemical fixing agent

Niddy Noddy Used for winding skeins

Noils Short fibres that are removed by combing

Orifice The hole at the end of the 'U' shaped flyer that the yarn goes through

Plying Two or more yarns spun together in the opposite direction to become a single yarn

Prime The part of the fleece which takes the worst of the weather and is often thin and dry

Rolag Made by carding fibres, the fibres are rolled into a tube and spun into a woollen yarn

Roving A fine, even fibre that has been combed and drawn out by hand, then slightly twisted before being spun into a worsted yarn

Saxony wheel Flyer type spinning wheel

Semi-worsted A yarn that is not true woollen or worsted

Scotch tension A nylon thread/band that controls the tension on a single band treadle wheel

Scouring Washing to remove the dirt and grease from a fleece

Shaft The spindle which has a whorl attached

Single A single yarn spun from a prepared fleece

Skein A hank of wool

Skirting Very short, dirty wool around the belly, and the legs - these should be removed and discarded

Sliver carded Wool that has not been made into a rolag, but left in a flat parrallel line

Slub Areas along the spun yarn that have little or no twist. This can be intentional, or a fault when an even yarn is needed

Sorting Dividing up the fleece into different parts

Spindle The middle of the 'U' shaped flyer where the bobbin is positioned

Staple A lock from a fleece - tip to root

S Twist Yarn spun in an anticlockwise direction

Suint Comes from the sheep glands and becomes hard at different times of the year

Teasing Opening up the fibres by hand or by combing

Teasles Used for combing locks before hand carders were invented

Top Commercially carded and combed fibre that has had the noils removed before being left in a parallel state to be spun into smooth yarn

Tuppings Marks on the back of the ewe left by the ram

Warp Threads that run lengthwise on a loom

Weft The yarn that runs across the loom using a shuttle

Wether A castrated sheep

Whorl A circular weight found at the base of the drop spindle

Woollen yarn Yarn spun from short carded fibres into the long draw style using a rolag

Worsted yarn Spun from fibres 7cm (3 inches) or more in length that have been combed and have had the noils removed, then spun in a parallel direction to make a smooth yarn

Z twist A yarn spun as a single in a clockwise direction

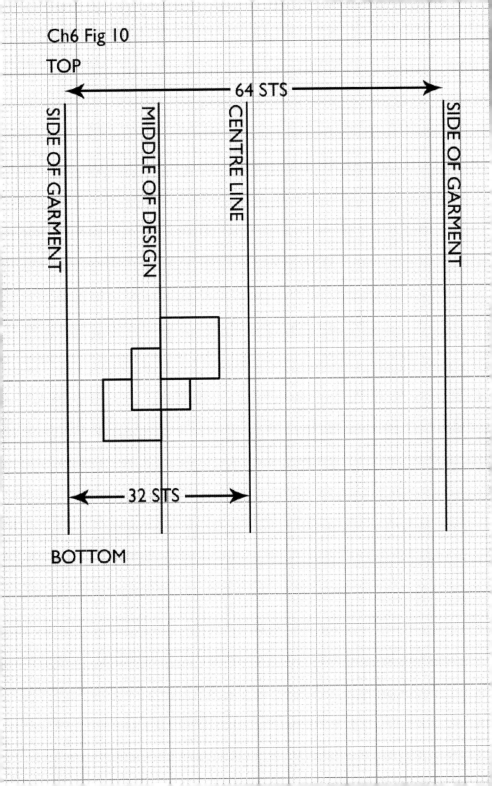

Ch6 Fig 10

TOP

← 64 STS →

SIDE OF GARMENT

MIDDLE OF DESIGN

CENTRE LINE

SIDE OF GARMENT

← 32 STS →

BOTTOM

INDEX

INDEX

SUPPLIERS

British Wool Marketing Board
Wool House,
Roydsdale Way,
Euroway Trading Estate
Bradford
Yorkshire BD4 6SE
Fleece
Tel: 01274 688666
www.britishwool.org.uk

John Arborn Textiles
Cold Harbour Mill
Uffculme
Devon
Craft books on hand spinning, alpaca and wool tops for sale and fleece commercially spun to order.
Tel: 01884 841442 (shop)
www.jarborn.com

Frank Herring & Sons
High Street
Dorchester
Dorset DT1 1UP
Spinning wheels and looms, fibres for hand spinning, mordants and natural dyes.
Tel: 01305 26449
www.frankherringandsons.com

P & M Wool Crafts & Ashill Dyes
Pindon End Cottage
Pindon End
Hanslope
Milton Keynes
Bucks. MK19 7 HN
Books, fleece, natural dyes and mordants.
Tel: 01908510277
www.naturaldyes.co.uk

Whorl Drop Spindles
Kevin Rhodes
12 Carr Lane
Kirkham
Lancs.
Spindles in different woods
Tel: 01772 9786466
Email: Kevin@whorldropspindle.co.uk

Wingham Wool Work
70 Main Street
Wentworth
Rotherham
South Yorkshire
S62 7TN
Spinning equipment, commercial tops, fleece and courses
Tel: 01226 742926
Email winghamwoolwork.co.uk

The Good Life Press Ltd.
The Old Pigsties
Clifton Fields
Lytham Road
Preston
PR4 0XG
A wide range of books on many rural crafts from spinning and food to sheep and other animal husbandry and the magazine Home Farmer which encourages the reader to take up these crafts from their own home.
Tel: 01772 633444
www.goodlifepress.co.uk
www.homefarmer.co.uk